How to plan radio adve

By the same author

Running a Successful Advertising Campaign
How to Plan Press Advertising
How to Plan Exhibitions
How to Plan Direct Mail
The Perfect Conference
The Business Planner
Business Planning Made Simple
Successful Business Plans in a Week
Correct Letters
Instant Business Letters
Write That Letter!
Tricky Business Forms
Budgeting for Non-financial Managers

How to plan radio advertising

Iain Maitland

CASSELL

Cassell

Wellington House, 125 Strand, London WC2R 0BB

127 West 24th Street, New York, NY 10011

First published 1996

British Library Cataloguing-in-Publication Data
A catalogue record for this book is available from the British Library.

ISBN 0-304-33429-4

Designed and typeset by Kenneth Burnley at Irby, Wirral, Cheshire.
Printed and bound in Great Britain by Redwood Books, Trowbridge, Wilts.

Contents

Acknowledgements

I WISH TO ACKNOWLEDGE the help of the following organizations which provided information or assistance in the compilation of this book. Special thanks to those which allowed me to reproduce their material in the text:

Abbot Mead Vickers–BBDO Ltd, and Malcolm Duffy in particular.
The Advertising Association
The Association of Independent Radio Companies Limited
The Broadcasting Standards Council
Capital Radio
Classic FM
Maclean Hunter Limited, and Clare Thomas in particular
The Radio Advertising Bureau Limited
The Radio Authority, and Tony Stoller in particular
The Radio Sales Company
Radio Trent
Scottish and Irish Radio Sales
Suffolk Group Radio plc, and Robb Young in particular

To Tracey, Michael and Sophie

Preface

How to Plan Radio Advertising is for you – the owner or manager of a prospective, new or existing small business who is planning to advertise over the airwaves, perhaps for the first time. The book starts by introducing radio as an advertising medium. 'Types of radio station' states the characteristics of radio stations as well as the advantages and disadvantages of advertising on them. 'Who's who in radio' goes inside a radio station and also explains the varied roles of radio bodies and advertising organizations.

Next, it describes the preliminary work which will help you to decide if the radio is an appropriate advertising medium for your firm, whilst giving you the information needed to make the correct choices during any consequent advertising activities. 'Evaluating your business' covers looking at your concern, studying goods and services and clarifying your targets. 'Understanding the marketplace' tells you how to consider your customers, think about your rivals, view the market and fill in the gaps in your knowledge as and where relevant.

Moving ahead, the text takes you step-by-step up to a radio advertising campaign, to ensure that the right decisions are made at each stage. 'Fixing an appropriation' discusses analysing sales, appraising profits and contemplating other factors before allocating a suitable budget. 'Planning your activities' shows you how to approach radio stations, peruse rate cards, assess audiences, calculate costs and prepare your schedule of advertisements.

Then, the book works through your initial advertising activities on the radio. 'Composing advertisements' examines selecting your approach, choosing contents and the vitally important subject of complying with the law in this area. 'Running your campaign' details how to purchase airtime, conduct a trial run to judge your activities and amend your schedule accordingly. 'The radio advertiser's checklist' offers you the opportunity to review every task in turn to spot successes and remedy errors.

Appendices are incorporated at the end of the text. Data about independent radio stations, reproduced rate cards, extracts from the Code of Advertising Standards and Practice plus lists of useful contacts and recommended reading join together to form a comprehensive and valuable reference section. When linked with the action checklists, chapter summaries and the glossary of key terms, this material helps to make the book a practical and thorough guide to radio advertising, now and in the future.

Iain Maitland

1 Types of radio station

THERE ARE MORE THAN two hundred independent radio stations in the United Kingdom, ranging from Plymouth Sound in England to Heartland FM in Scotland, Downtown Radio in Northern Ireland and Swansea Sound in Wales. As an advertising medium, commercial radio offers a unique blend of characteristics, advantages and disadvantages to its advertisers. To begin with, you should be broadly familiar with these key features before going on to decide whether radio advertising is right for your firm and – if it is – to run a successful advertising campaign over the airwaves.

Characteristics of radio stations

The late 1980s and early 1990s have seen enormous and unprecedented changes taking place both in the BBC and commercial radio. The long-term future of the BBC is under discussion and review, and if at some stage the corporation decides to accept advertising, this will be of enormous interest to prospective advertisers. Independent radio has been deregulated, with the removal of innumerable restrictions enabling more and more stations to be set up. In 1990 – when deregulation was initiated by statute – 107 commercial radio stations existed. With thirty or so new ones currently entering the marketplace each year, over three hundred are expected to be broadcasting by the late 1990s.

Independent radio – of prime concern to advertisers – is not only increasing in size, but changing in shape too, evolving from a purely local medium into a local, regional *and* national one as the 1990s unfold. Local stations such as Invicta Radio in Kent and Manx Radio on the Isle of Man continue to serve community needs whilst proliferating in numbers to cater for previously uncovered areas. Five regional stations look likely to be established during the decade, in Central Scotland, North East England, North West England, the West Midlands plus South Wales and Avon. National commercial radio stations now exist too, such as Classic FM, Talk Radio and Virgin, with others to follow.

Not surprisingly, each of these stations has its own unique personality. Local radio stations – which will probably continue to receive the vast bulk of radio advertising expenditure for some time to come – are traditionally a mix of music, news, phone-ins, competitions, sports, traffic, travel, weather and other reports, all geared up to meet the requirements of their individual audiences, whether rural or urban. Devon Air in the sleepy South West has a different flavour to Capital FM in busy London. They both reflect their own particular communities, and do it well. Regional stations are expected to be distinct from local stations in their areas – a difficult if not impossible task – and might concentrate on particular forms of music as the independent national stations do, with Classic FM's classical music, Virgin's rock music and so on.

The burgeoning numbers and types of radio stations are (and will be) transmitted on FM and AM wavebands, or 'VHF' and 'medium wave' as they were once more commonly known. The FM band extends in frequency from 87.7 MHz to 108.0 MHz. FM 87.5 to 94.6 MHz is used mainly by BBC regional and national radio; 94.6 to 96.1 MHz by BBC local radio and BBC Radio 4 in places; 96.1 to 97.6 MHz by independent local radio; 97.6 to 99.8 MHz by BBC Radio 4; 99.8 to 102.0 MHz by independent local and national radio;102.0 to 103.5 MHz by independent local radio; and 103.5 to 105.0 MHz by BBC local radio. The AM band spans 531 kHz to 1602 kHz, comprising BBC and independent local and regional transmissions with some BBC national services too.

Audience numbers for radio stations vary significantly. In terms of total population, a local station such as Classic Trax in Belfast can be heard by up to 540,000 people, whereas Kiss 100 FM in London covers 9,700,000, which is likely to be on a par with some regional radio stations. Independent national stations may be picked up by all (or almost all) of the 55 million population. Most reputable radio stations will provide (independently audited) figures of their estimated weekly audience, or 'reach'. As examples, Classic Trax 'reaches' 32,000 or 6 per cent of its target population and Kiss 100 FM 'reaches' 1,091,000 or 11 per cent.

The types of people who listen to commercial radio stations differ considerably too; the long-held (and once partially correct) belief that only 15- to 24-year-olds tune in is no longer sustainable and audiences are changing as rapidly as independent radio itself. Most quality radio stations supply independently verified figures breaking down their audience into various groupings, typically by sex, age (5 to 14 years, 15 to 24 years, 25 to 34 years, 35 to 54 years, 55 years plus) and social class (A: upper middle class, B: middle class, C1: lower middle class, C2: skilled working class, D: working class, E: those on lowest subsistence levels such as pensioners). As a general rule, commercial radio now appeals to a broader cross-section of the population. For example Southern FM on the Sussex coast plays classic hits, and its audience make-up or 'profile' is 50 per cent male, 50 per cent female, 23 per cent 15 to 24 years, 57 per cent 25 to 54 years and 20 per cent 55 years plus. 53 per cent are ABC1s and 47 per cent are C2DEs .

Listening habits follow similar patterns in many respects. The typical household – so far as one exists – has some three to four radios around the home, which are usually tuned in to just one or two favoured stations. The radio audience normally peaks at breakfast time with all types of people listening around the house and then falls steadily away throughout the day, as listeners go to work, do the shopping, see friends, or whatever. The stay-at-home audience of housewives, young children, students, the unemployed, pensioners and the like is boosted briefly at teatime as people return home from work before reducing again into the evening. Saturday and Sunday listening patterns, perhaps surprisingly, follow closely matching trends. On average, the radio listener tunes in for between seven and twelve hours per week.

So far as radio advertising is concerned, airtime is sold on a 'spot' basis, typically of thirty seconds' duration. The cost of each spot varies according to when it is transmitted, with the day divided into segments and priced in relation to the audience during that period. As an example, SGR FM in Suffolk charges £54 per thirty-second spot between 6 a.m. and noon, £32 between noon and 6 p.m. and £14 between 6 p.m. and midnight. Shorter and longer spots are available, on request. Ten- and twenty-second spots on SGR FM are respectively 50 and 20 per cent less than the equivalent thirty-second spot. Forty-, fifty- and sixty-second spots are 30, 65 and 80 per cent more than the relevant thirty-second spot. Advertisements which are longer than sixty seconds are charged pro rata to the sixty-second rate.

Normally, a package of advertisements is purchased, perhaps twenty-eight over one week, 112 over four weeks, 196 over seven weeks, 364 over thirteen weeks and so forth. Obviously, the more airtime bought, the lower the average price per spot. Volume, advance booking, first-time and other assorted discounts – ranging between 5 and 25 per cent according to circumstances – are nearly always on offer to entice advertisers. Spots are usually distributed evenly throughout each week and day unless otherwise agreed. Early-week discounts of 20 to 30 per cent may be given for advertising only on Sundays Mondays and Tuesdays, with end-of-week surcharges of the same amounts applying for Thursday, Friday and Saturday advertising. Limiting transmissions to a particular day might increase costs by 10 per cent, to a specific hour by 20 per cent, to a day *and* hour by 30 per cent and to a given break by 50 per cent.

Independent radio stations – small or large, in the country or in the city – provide in-house production facilities, whereby advertisements are scripted and produced by them for a set fee, subject to advertisers' suggestions and requests. For example, Orchard FM based in Taunton in Somerset charges £85 for a basic commercial, comprising one voice-over plus a piece of music or sound effect. Each additional voice – perhaps as heard in a so-called customers' conversation about the merits of a business or a product – costs £23.50. Extra music and/or sound effects are charged at £25 and £15 respectively, per piece or per effect. Whether a small venture or a multinational, advertisers receive the same service.

Advantages of radio advertising

Radio is a varied and diverse advertising medium, offering considerable choice to its advertisers, who may advertise via one or more than a hundred stations, on a local, regional or national basis and alongside jazz, the classics or middle-of-the-road music. They can advertise at different times of the year, month, week, day or night, and as frequently or as infrequently as they wish. Advertisements may differ from one station to another, from morning to night or even from transmission to transmission – all of which helps advertisers to ensure that the right numbers and types of listeners receive the right messages at the right times and places.

Radio is also both immediate and responsive to advertisers' needs. Albeit carefully timed and scripted in most cases, it usually broadcasts live amid potentially changing circumstances with news being made and events unfolding on air. It therefore has a fresh and topical feel which may rub off on those businesses advertising on it. Similarly, radio stations can react quickly to their advertisers' requirements with advertisements written, cleared, recorded and transmitted in hours when necessary, allowing advertisers to respond to changes in the marketplace, keeping abreast of the competition and remaining up to date in the eyes of their customers.

Despite the dramatic developments occurring in the radio industry, commercial radio is still – and will probably stay for some time yet – a predominantly local medium, identifying with and moulding itself to the needs and wants of its specific audience, whether in the Welsh Valleys or the Scottish Highlands. It is often regarded as almost a companion by many listeners, and as being friendly and approachable, trustworthy and reliable. Again, those small firms which advertise via this medium – perhaps promoting themselves as on-the-spot businesses with similar qualities to those believed to be possessed by the radio station – may find that they are perceived in the same way by the audience.

Radio is also physically compact and therefore portable, unlike other media such as television. It can be heard in the home, whether in the bedroom, bathroom, kitchen or lounge. It may be listened to in the car or on the train, when travelling to work. It can be carried out into the garden, to break up the monotony of mowing the lawn or the drudgery of weeding the flowerbeds. Whenever one chooses to advertise, wherever the listeners are and whatever they are doing when advertisements are transmitted, they can potentially be reached at all times and in all situations.

With thirty seconds of airtime purchased for as little as £10 to £15 and an advertisement created for under £100, radio is an inexpensive advertising medium to use, in terms of both airtime costs and production expenses. Thus, small firms can not only afford to advertise on it but are able to do so extensively and regularly. As important – if not more so – it allows smaller concerns to compete on a relatively equal footing with their national rivals, without being priced out of the most popular spots and outclassed by glossy production techniques as happens in other media, most notably television.

Disadvantages of radio advertising

As an advertising medium, radio has several, significant drawbacks that need to be considered carefully, and which could even dissuade advertisers from conducting a campaign over the airwaves. It is one-dimensional, wholly dependent upon sound for its success. Obviously, text, pictures, colours and so on – the key ingredients of most winning advertising media – simply do not exist in this medium, and advertisers must convey their messages through speech, music and sound effects. Clearly, this might not suit certain firms, goods, services and so forth. Even if it does, creating quality advertisements to be heard but not seen is a hard – sometimes near impossible – task.

Radio is also a transient medium, with advertisements going into one ear and out of the other within ten, twenty, thirty seconds, or whatever. It is hard to put across any message, let alone a complex or detailed one, in such a short time. Lengthening the advertisement to perhaps forty, fifty or sixty seconds, or broadcasting it more frequently may bore or irritate listeners, as well as increasing costs. Even if the message does register, other advertisements, a news update, traffic and travel information or another classic hit is then transmitted, demanding the listener's attention and interest.

Of course, radio is often little more than a background noise anyway, to be half-heard when boring tasks are being carried out, whether writing an essay, doing household chores, driving to work or filling in forms at the office. It may be listened to now and then for a news headline or favourite song but rarely has the listener's total concentration on an ongoing basis. When it does – for a lively phone-in or a chart show – listeners do not really want to hear the advertisements, which are tolerated until the next caller comes on the line or the next record is played. It is not unusual for some listeners to station-hop during advertisements, trying to find more music.

An unavoidable disadvantage that needs to be faced and considered is that the number of listeners tuning in to a radio station is usually fairly low in relation to the population covered by its transmission area. Consequently, the right types of listeners and potential customers reached are that much lower too.

This drawback could grow into one of over-riding significance as the decade progresses and more and more local, regional and national stations start broadcasting. The numbers of listeners and hours listened will not increase in the same proportions – if at all – which means that advertisers will probably find themselves advertising to a gradually shrinking audience per station.

Radio is also a hard-to-measure medium. It is difficult to know exactly who heard which advertisements and how they reacted to them. People responding to a newspaper advertisement may return a coupon or quote a reference number. Visitors to an exhibition stand might fill out an enquiry form, or be logged by stand staff. Customers replying to a sales letter from a firm will mention the letter or return an easily identified reply paid card. Radio listeners will most likely just telephone through an order or walk in and buy a product without indicating that they listened to and acted upon an advertisement. Advertisers will have to work hard to find out if their activities were effective.

Summary

1. There are more than two hundred independent radio stations in the United Kingdom. As an advertising medium, commercial radio offers a unique blend of:
   a) characteristics;
   b) advantages;
   c) disadvantages.

2. Independent radio has numerous, identifiable characteristics. In particular:
   a) the medium is increasing in size, and changing in shape;
   b) each radio station has its own individual personality;
   c) the medium transmits on FM and AM wavebands;
   d) audience numbers and types vary considerably from one station to another;
   e) listening habits tend to follow a similar pattern, whatever the radio station;
   f) airtime is sold on a spot basis, with a package of advertisements usually being purchased for a specific period;
   g) in-house production facilities are available for would-be advertisers at each radio station.

3. As an advertising medium, radio has several advantages:
   a) it is varied and diverse, and offers choice to its advertisers;
   b) it is immediate and responsive to advertisers' needs;

   c) it is predominantly a local medium, moulding itself to its listeners' requirements;

   d) it is portable, and can be heard anywhere;

   e) it is relatively inexpensive, and affordable by smaller firms.

4. Radio has various disadvantages too:

   a) it is one-dimensional, and wholly dependent on sound;

   b) it is a transient medium, with advertisements lasting for just a few seconds each;

   c) it is often a background noise, only half-listened to;

   d) the proportion of people within a transmission area who actually tune in to each radio station is fairly low;

   e) the increasing number of radio stations means that proportionally fewer people listen to each one;

   f) it is a hard-to-measure medium.

2 Who's who in radio

IF YOU ARE THINKING of advertising on radio, you should know about the various departments and employees inside a radio station as well as the radio bodies and advertising organizations which you might come across during your activities. It is sensible to be conscious of their roles within the radio and advertising industries and what they can do for you as a would-be radio advertiser using the medium for the first time.

Inside a radio station

It is useful to start by learning something about those departments and employees with whom you are most likely to come into contact at some stage of your advertising campaign. Naturally, each and every radio station is different in terms of size and structure, but most will contain the following, in one form or another:

- The Programming Department;
- The Sales Department;
- The Production Department;
- The Marketing Department;
- The Accounts Department.

The Progamming Department

Programming is responsible for interpreting and giving the listening audience what it wants to hear. It decides upon the mix of programmes that are transmitted, the presenters who front these programmes, the range of music played whether from the 1960s and 1970s or the latest chart sounds, and the overall blend of programmes, music, news and so on that actually goes on air. In practice, control may rest in the hands of the station owner – consequently known as the 'programme controller' – or a board of directors in larger concerns, perhaps representing each of the departments or functions involved within the station. In all probability, you will have little or nothing to do with these controllers, nor the presenters, journalists and secretaries working for them.

The Sales Department

The role of this department is to sell all of the advertising time available for each day, week and month, and for the best prices. The sales – or 'advertisement' – director, manager and executives usually work closely with programming to ensure that programmes, music and advertisements are well matched. For example, if programming is planning to broadcast a special, week-long feature on job hunting, executives would be despatched to attract suitable recruitment advertisers for that period. Similarly, a one-off programme on environmental issues might mean that firms with an interest in this subject would be approached for advertising. Usually, a sales or advertisement executive will act as a go-between, in your day-to-day dealings with the station throughout your campaign.

Many radio stations are also represented by independently owned sales houses which sell advertising time on their behalf, on a fee or commission basis. These sales – or 'rep' – houses are based in London and other big cities where larger advertisers and their advertising agencies are located, so that negotiations can be conducted more easily, face to face if required. As examples, Independent Radio Sales, and Media Sales and Marketing are based in London and Manchester. You may liaise with a representative of a sales house if you are sited in or near to a big city and wish to advertise via a distant, provincial station. See Chapter 6: 'Planning your activities', page 38 and Chapter 8: 'Running your campaign', page 70. Addresses and telephone numbers of sales houses are given in Appendix D: 'Useful contacts', page 140.

The Production Department

A production team – of sound engineers, technicians and the like – is responsible for putting the programmes, presenters and music on air, to be heard by the listening audience. Although you will almost certainly not deal directly with production staff, they will play a significant role in your advertising activities. As a small-business owner or manager without expertise in this field, they will inevitably transfer the thoughts and ideas that you have for your advertisements onto tape for transmission. Voice-overs will be done by a nucleus of actors used regularly, with music and sound effects being added from the station's music and sound effects library, built up over the years. Refer to Chapter 7: 'Composing advertisements', page 58.

The Marketing Department

Equally likely to be known as the promotions or advertising department – and incorporating market research and merchandizing functions – this has the key responsibility of publicizing the station in order to increase and expand its audience and advertisers, in terms of both numbers and types. The marketing manager and his or her team of assistants may do this in various ways. They will carry out market research into the station's transmission area and audience which will be made available to prospective advertisers. They may use direct mail shots and trade press advertisements to attract advertisers, and local and national press advertisements, sponsorship of events and the merchandizing of pens, pencils, cups and so on to increase awareness of the station amongst its potential audience. Various facts and figures will be given to you either through the station's rate card or via a sales executive, when you eventually meet one. See Chapter 6: 'Planning your activities', page 38, and Chapter 8: 'Running your campaign', page 70.

The Accounts Department

As with all organizations, a radio station has an accounts department to handle financial and associated administrative matters, issuing invoices, paying bills and so forth. Since most of your advertising activities will be dealt with by a sales executive acting for you, it is likely that you will not come across this department or its staff until later on in your campaign when invoices are issued. You would be advised to check these carefully, as mistakes can and often do arise at this stage. Refer to Chapter 8: 'Running your campaign', page 70.

Radio bodies

Various trade bodies exist which represent, monitor and/or regulate the different organizations working within the radio industry. You should be aware of these, what they do and how they can help you to become a more successful advertiser within this particular medium. See Appendix D: 'Useful contacts', page 140 for relevant addresses and telephone numbers:

- The Association of Independent Radio Companies Limited;
- The Broadcasting Standards Council;
- The Radio Advertising Bureau Limited;
- The Radio Authority;
- Radio Joint Audience Research.

The Association of Independent Radio Companies Limited

AIRC is the trade association of commercial radio stations in the United Kingdom, with a membership of all but a handful of the smaller stations. Widely recognized as one of the most active and effective bodies in the media world, it represents its members in dealings with the government and the regulatory organization known as the Radio Authority as well as maintaining close and constructive links with fellow trade and advertising associations, other broad-casting bodies such as the BBC and overseas radio stations. Of prime interest to advertisers, it manages research on behalf of Radio Joint Audience Research, provides a script clearance and advisory system for what can and cannot be included in radio advertisements, and is the central source of radio information in the country. See Chapter 7: 'Composing advertisements, page 58 and Appendix C: 'Code of Advertising Standards and Practice', page 117 .

The Broadcasting Standards Council

The Council is an independent body acting on behalf of consumers in the United Kingdom. Its brief is to deal with the range of issues arising from the portrayal of sexual conduct and violence, and matters of taste and decency relating to television and radio programmes and advertisements. It monitors programmes and advertisements on an ongoing basis, conducts research into audience opinions and attitudes, provides a forum for consumer discussions through public meetings and correspondence, and considers complaints from consumers. It prefers to adopt an advisory role – of relevance to would-be advertisers – rather than a regulatory one, although it does possess certain statutory powers, such as compelling offending programmes to broadcast its findings.

The Radio Advertising Bureau Limited

The RAB is a small company supported financially by all of the independent radio stations in the United Kingdom, with a board of directors drawn from just six leading stations in order to shorten decision-making processes. Its aims are to mount studies into how radio advertising works, to correct widely held prejudices about the medium, to build up a database of radio advertising experiences to share with potential advertisers, and to promote radio as an advertising medium. Along with AIRC, this is probably your best source of advice and guidance on all aspects of your radio advertising campaign, from start to finish.

The Radio Authority

This authority licenses and regulates the independent radio industry in the United Kingdom. Its over-riding aim is to help to develop and grow a successful and diverse radio network throughout the country which offers a wide listening choice to the whole population. It plans frequencies, awards licences to radio stations, regulates programmes and advertising as necessary, and plays a key role in discussing and formulating policies which affect the independent radio world and its listeners. Of significance to prospective advertisers, it publishes the Code of Advertising Standards and Practice (and Programme Sponsorship) that sets the standards to which stations and advertisers must adhere at all times. See Chapter 7: 'Composing Advertisements', page 58, and Appendix C: 'Code of Advertising Standards and Practice', page 117, for further details.

Radio Joint Audience Research

RAJAR is a limited company owned jointly by the BBC and AIRC with a management committee made up of representatives of other radio and advertising organizations that is responsible for supervising research into the listening habits of audiences tuning in to BBC and independent radio stations. It was created in 1992 to replace the Joint Industry Committee for Radio Audience Research – JICRAR for short – which performed the same, basic function but for the independent network only. The BBC had also commissioned its own research surveys up to that stage, producing findings that sometimes conflicted with those generated by JICRAR. To avoid such contrasting figures, the two parties decided to form RAJAR to produce unified results for the whole industry.

The research system evolving through RAJAR – with its first findings published in 1993 and adopted steadily by radio stations thereafter – is essentially the same as the well-known JICRAR one, but more detailed. A representative sample of households throughout the country completes weekly diaries showing its listening habits in quarter-hour periods. From these diaries, projections are made to show total numbers and types of audience per station and at different times, cumulative weekly audiences, total and average listening hours and so on, the key details of which are given in radio stations' promotional literature. Refer to Chapter 6: 'Planning your activities', page 38, and Appendix B: 'Rate cards', page 95.

Advertising organizations

Several other organizations are directly or indirectly involved with radio advertising, representing and advising key participants within the industry. Addresses and phone numbers are set out in Appendix D: 'Useful contacts', page 140:

- The Advertising Association;
- The Association of Media Independents Limited;
- The Incorporated Society of British Advertisers Limited;
- The Institute of Practitioners in Advertising.

The Advertising Association

The AA has a membership consisting of trade associations and professional bodies acting on behalf of media owners, advertisers, advertising agencies, media independents and miscellaneous organizations which supply associated services. Its aims are to protect the interests of its members, improve advertising standards, increase confidence in and broaden and deepen universal understanding of advertising and its place in the economic and social framework. The Association can provide advertisers with data on all aspects of advertising including preparing for, conducting and appraising a radio campaign.

The Association of Media Independents Limited

The AMI acts for those specialist companies which are concerned solely with the planning, buying and evaluation of media, rather than in the creation and design of advertisements as well. The Association stipulates that its members must be of sound professional status, totally independent of media owners, advertisers and advertising agencies, financially stable and in the business of media purchasing only. Thus, those firms which wish to join AMI have to be recognized by all of the major media owner bodies, such as AIRC. They need to show their client lists and billing information to verify their capabilities across all types of media. Also, they have to provide a written undertaking to supply their customers with copy invoices from appropriate media, highlighting the costs of time and space bought by them. Accounts need to be submitted too, as proof of financial independence and standing. It can provide general advice on running an advertising campaign.

The Incorporated Society of British Advertisers Limited

This society represents national and international advertisers of all sizes, and from all trades and industries. It seeks to advance the interests of its members in discussions with the media and its associations, the government and other official organizations involved with advertising matters. It tries to assist prospective radio advertisers to advertise more successfully on air, by offering them advice and guidance as and when required on areas as diverse as market research, composing advertisements and administering a campaign.

The Institute of Practitioners in Advertising

The IPA acts on behalf of advertising agencies in the United Kingdom, providing its membership with help and suggestions and promoting their viewpoints in liaison with the government, media bodies and the advertising industry. The Institute demands that its members are able to plan and carry out advertising campaigns from beginning to end. Therefore, only full service agencies and not media independents are eligible to join the IPA. To ensure that this rule is met, the Institute assesses each applicant's experience by looking at its client base and the type, number and variety of accounts handled. Financial status, creditworthiness and recognition by other professional associations are taken into account as well. Again, the IPA may offer you information and assistance on advertising, if approached.

Summary

1. Prospective radio advertisers should be aware of who's who within the industry. Most notably, they need to know about:
   a) the departments and employees inside a radio station;
   b) radio bodies;
   c) other advertising organizations.

2. When dealing with a radio station, most advertisers will come into contact with:
   a) the programming department;
   b) the sales department;
   c) the production department;
   d) the marketing department;
   e) the accounts department.

3. Various trade bodies exist within the radio industry, and include:
   a) The Association of Independent Radio Companies Limited;
   b) The Broadcasting Standards Council;
   c) The Radio Advertising Bureau Limited;
   d) The Radio Authority;
   e) Radio Joint Audience Research.

4. Other advertising organizations have a role to play within the radio industry. In particular:
   a) The Advertising Association;
   b) The Association of Media Independents Limited;
   c) The Incorporated Society of British Advertisers Limited;
   d) The Institute of Practitioners in Advertising.

3 Evaluating your business

HAVING BUILT UP a general understanding of the radio industry, it is wise to spend some time looking at your concern and its goods, services and targets. By studying these in considerable breadth and depth, it may become apparent that radio is an inappropriate advertising medium in your circumstances, thus saving you from wasting time and money on what would ultimately prove to be unrewarding activities. If your company's activities still seem suited to radio advertising, however, all your accumulated knowledge of the business will stand you in good stead during any subsequent campaign, providing you with the information needed to help you to make the right choices and decisions at key moments.

Looking at your concern

Analyse your firm as fully as you can. How is it organized? What does it do? Consider your business premises. How large are they? What facilities are available? What type of image do they convey to the outside world? Think about the location of your concern. Why is it based there? Is it well located? For whom? What else is sited nearby? Check out the various departments within your firm, if appropriate. What is happening in them? Who is doing what? Talk to your colleagues and employees. What can they tell you about the business that you do not already know? Keep watching, asking and listening to develop a complete and accurate picture of the structure and activities of your organization, from top to bottom.

Make a careful note of all the positive features of your firm, as confirmed or revealed during your investigations. Perhaps your list may incorporate statements along the lines of: It is a long-established, family-run concern with a good reputation in the locality; as a small, hands-on business, we can respond quickly to changing and developing circumstances, whatever their nature; our property is spacious and well designed, and has a car park, refreshment and washroom facilities for customers; it is located in a central position, easily reached by and accessible to our customers; we have a pleasant and experienced sales team who serve customers in a warm and efficient manner; and so on.

Then set out any negative features which could be associated with your concern, as substantiated or uncovered in the course of your examination. Your comments might include: Like most smaller firms, we operate with limited resources at our disposal which restrict us in many ways; we cannot afford to buy goods in bulk as larger companies do, and are thus unable to compete with them in terms of price; we lack the finances to spend substantial sums on advertising, and must make every pound count; we do not possess specialized marketing and advertising skills and experience as bigger businesses do, and have to use our common sense when planning any activities; and so forth.

A detailed awareness of all aspects of your firm, together with an appreciation of radio, should enable you to draw some preliminary conclusions about the suitability of advertising over the airwaves. Referring to these specific statements and comments as an example, you might decide that radio is a potentially fitting medium, worth further thought and consideration in this instance. Independent radio stations do allow family-run businesses to promote their established image within the local community, and to swiftly announce their responses to changing scenarios, whether in the form of new stock deliveries, price cuts, clearance sales or whatever. Such advertising can be carried out at relatively low cost, which suits firms trading with limited financial resources, and in-house advice can be given and production facilities used to help advertisers to overcome a lack of knowledge in this field. You may find it helpful at this stage to complete 'Looking at your concern: an action checklist' on page 17.

Studying goods and services

Assess your products as far as possible. What goods do you produce and/or sell? What types and varieties exist? Are they top quality products? What do they look like? What are their uses? Are they reliable? Are they safe? What are their prices? Are the goods readily available? What guarantees are attached to them? Contemplate your services too. What services do you offer? What exactly do they involve? How good are they? How often do they need to be carried out? How much do they cost? Always make certain that you are wholly familiar with both your products and your services, knowing them inside and out.

Evaluating each product and service one after another, write down their individual strengths, as seen from the customers' viewpoints. For example, your list of pluses for a key product might incorporate these comments: It is handmade to an extremely high standard by skilled craftspeople working in our own workshops; with its unique design, its appearance distinguishes it from comparable, rival items; it offers the widest variety of colours in today's marketplace; it has several uses, which are not always immediately apparent until the product is fully demonstrated; and so on.

THE BUSINESS

Characteristics	Its positive features	Its negative features
1. Structure		
2. Activities		
3. Premises		
4. Facilities		
5. Location		
6. Surroundings		
7. Departments		
8. Employees		
9. Other aspects		

RADIO

Characteristics:

Advantages:

Disadvantages:

Looking at your concern: an action checklist

Sketch out any obvious weaknesses that you can identify, again adopting the customers' stance for your assessment. As an example, you could note the following minuses: given its specialized nature, production times are relatively lengthy; due to the expertise required during the manufacturing process and the shortage of skilled labour, our production capabilities are severely restricted; it is expensive in relation to competing goods in the market; it is not always available to customers as and when needed; and so forth.

Perusing your in-depth notes should allow you to think further about the relevance of radio as an advertising medium in the circumstances. Taking these comments as a specific example, the quality of the product, its unique design and the range of colours available cannot be shown over the radio, nor can the product's varied uses be demonstrated. Clearly, this is a huge and perhaps insurmountable drawback which needs to be considered carefully. Also, extensive radio advertising may generate a significant number of enquiries and orders which could not necessarily be met in time, bearing in mind the firm's limited production facilities. Refer to 'Studying goods and services: an action checklist' on page 19 for further assistance.

Clarifying your targets

Be absolutely clear about your overall business objectives, knowing precisely what you want to achieve in the coming months and years, and by when. For the immediate future over the next twelve months, you might jot down assorted goals such as these:

- We want to raise awareness of our concern, products and services within our trading region;
- We wish to generate enquiries about our goods and services from that area;
- We would like to double our customer base within the forthcoming year;
- We want to boost sales by the same amount over that period;
- We wish to steady sales demand, levelling off uneconomic peaks and troughs; and so on.

Your medium-term goals for the following two years or so could be to: remind existing customers of the various qualities of our firm, goods and services so that they buy from us again and again; notify relevant changes in our concern and product and service developments as and when appropriate; recruit suitable numbers and types of staff in preparation for market expansion; increase understanding of our business, goals and services across the north-east of the country, trebling enquiries, customer numbers and turnover during the twenty-four-month period; and so forth.

GOODS/SERVICES

Characteristics	Their strengths	Their weaknesses
1. Types		
2. Varieties		
3. Quality		
4. Appearance		
5. Uses		
6. Reliability		
7. Safety		
8. Prices		
9. Availability		
10. Guarantees		

RADIO

Characteristics:

Benefits:

Drawbacks:

Studying goods and services: an action checklist

In the long term, your targets might incorporate these: we wish to clear outdated products and services from our range before they decline in popularity; we want to develop and launch new and improved goods and services onto the markeplace as and when relevant; we would like to broaden recognition of our business and its products and services throughout the United Kingdom, raising enquiries, customer numbers and sales tenfold during a five-year period; we wish to work ourselves into a position to expand into overseas markets in due course.

Focusing sharply upon your over-riding goals does provide you with another opportunity to consider whether advertising on air is likely to help you in achieving the varied aims. With these particular objectives in mind, you can see that the projected local, regional and national expansion over one, three and five years could be assisted by spreading radio advertising from one local station to a regional one and on to one of the independent national radio stations in due course. Knowing what you want to do and when, also gives you a framework to work within and towards if you begin to advertise on the radio. You may find it useful to fill in 'Clarifying your targets: an action checklist' on page 21, at this point.

Summary

1. Would-be radio advertisers should spend some time studying their concern, goods, services and targets. This will enable them to:
   a) decide whether or not radio is an appropriate advertising medium in their situation;
   b) produce relevant notes of invaluable use later on if they proceed to advertise via radio.

2. When looking at their concern, it is sensible to:
   a) analyse all aspects of the firm, and as fully as possible;
   b) make a note of its positive features;
   c) record its various negative features;
   d) compare and contrast the firm and its positive and negative features with radio, to assess its suitability as an advertising medium.

3. Goods and services sold and provided must be assessed too, with particular attention being paid to:
   a) their key features;
   b) their individual strengths;
   c) their specific weaknesses;
   d) their relationship to radio as an advertising medium.

RADIO

Characteristics:

Pros:

Cons:

YOUR BUSINESS

Short-term targets	Medium-term targets	Long-term targets
1.		
2.		
3.		
4.		
5.		
6.		
7.		
8.		
9.		

Clarifying your targets: an action checklist

4. When studying their targets, it is advisable to categorize these with regard to:
   a) the short term;
   b) the medium term;
   c) the long term;
   d) radio as an advertising medium in these circumstances.

4 Understanding the marketplace

CONTINUING WITH YOUR preliminary work, you should now conduct a thorough analysis of your trading environment, considering your customers, thinking about your rivals, viewing the market and filling in the gaps in your knowledge through research activities. As with your self-assessment, such an in-depth examination ought to indicate whether the radio is likely to be a suitable or unsuitable advertising medium in this particular instance. Should it seem fitting, you will have expanded your background knowledge of your overall circumstances and acquired additional notes for subsequent reference and assistance during any radio advertising campaign.

Considering your customers

Discover all you can about your customers, trying to create a concise picture of your 'typical' customer if you deal with too many businesses and/or individuals, for one-by-one evaluation. Contemplate fellow concerns, if relevant. How many do you trade with? Where are they based? What do they do? Who are the key decision-makers within the firms? What are these people like? Think about those members of the public who may be your customers, if appropriate. How many of them are there? Where do they live? Where do they work? Are they male or female? What are their ages? What social grades might be best associated with them? ABC1? C2DE? See what other information can be uncovered. Are they married or single? Do they have children? What are their occupations? How much do they earn? What interests do they have?

It is also wise to find out as much as possible about their various thoughts and opinions. What do they think of your firm, goods and services? What do they perceive to be strengths and weaknesses? What are their views of your competitors, rival products and services, and their 'pluses and minuses'? Check on their buying habits. What goods do they purchase? Which services do they use? When do they buy products and/or use services, and how often? Where do they purchase goods and/or use services, if not from you? If you can, learn about their radio listening habits as well. Which stations do they tune in to, and why? When do they listen? What do they do whilst the radio is on? How often do they tune in? How long do they listen for?

Having reviewed your business records, talked to colleagues and employees and approached customers as and when necessary, you should be able to piece together answers to these questions. Then you can consider the relevance of radio in relation to your customer base. As examples, trading with a limited number of known customers suggests that the use of an advertising medium such as radio which reaches large numbers of unknown people scattered over a wide area is inappropriate. Other media such as direct mail might be more relevant. Likewise, by simply finding out at this early stage that the majority of your customers do not even listen to the radio will save you a considerable amount of wasted time and money – a seemingly obvious point, but one which is overlooked time and time again by first-time advertisers in the medium. See 'Considering your customers: an action checklist' on page 25. Completing it may be beneficial to you.

Thinking about your rivals

Investigate your competitors as extensively as possible. How are they structured? What are their properties like? Are they well sited? How many departments and employees do they have? Are quality staff employed? What are the positive and negative features, as seen through customers' eyes? How do they compare and contrast with your firm? Look at their goods and services too. What exactly do they sell to the customers? What are these products and services like? What are their strengths and weaknesses, as far as customers are concerned? How do you feel they compare to or differ from your own range of goods and services?

Also consider any past and/or present advertising activities conducted by your various rivals over the airwaves. Have they ever used this medium so far as you are aware? If 'Yes', why do you think they chose it? Which particular characteristics of the radio most suited them? If 'No', why do you believe they have avoided it? What were the drawbacks of the medium that dissuaded them from advertising on it? As far as you can tell – and it is not easy unless you listen to each radio station all day and every day – try to build up an understanding of their campaigns. On which stations do they advertise, and when? How often are their advertisements transmitted? How long do they last for? What are the advertisements like? What precisely do they say? How do they say it?

Once more, you can think about radio in the light of what you have learned of your rivals. Clearly, those successful competitors which regularly use this advertising medium must do so with good reason, presumably because it helps them to achieve their goals, whether to increase enquiries, raise sales or

BUSINESSES	RADIO	INDIVIDUALS	RADIO
1. Numbers	Characteristics:	1. Numbers	Characteristics:
2. Locations		2. Locations	
3. Activities		3. Sexes	
4. Decision makers	Strengths:	4. Ages	Strengths:
5. Types		5. Social grades	
6. Thoughts/opinions		6. Thoughts/opinions	
7. Buying habits	Weaknesses:	7. Buying habits	Weaknesses:
8. Listening habits		8. Listening habits	

Considering your customers: an action checklist

whatever. Assuming that you compare more than contrast with them – perhaps in terms of size, products, services and so on – you may feel that it would be equally rewarding for you to promote yourself on air too. Knowing that they advertise on one station but not another, at this but not that time for example, will also be useful when you set about scheduling your own campaign in due course. 'Thinking about your rivals: an action checklist' on page 27 could help you to clarify your thoughts in this area.

Viewing the market

Familiarize yourself with the marketplace in which you operate, or intend to expand into in the near future. What is its size? What is its total annual turnover? Think about how it is organized and administered. What representative associations exist? Which roles do they adopt? Which functions do they perform? What regulatory bodies monitor the industry? What exactly do they do? Consider the other organizations that are in the market. What manufacturers, wholesalers and retailers trade in the industry? What are their individual market shares? How do they all mix and work together? How does your own firm fit into the marketplace?

It is also sensible to contemplate the influences upon the market. Take account of political activities and economic movements. How might government policies affect your marketplace? What about rising or falling interest rates, and inflation? Are exchange rates a significant factor? Consider social and demographic trends. Does public opinion have a major impact, and how? What about a growing and ageing population? How about increasing or decreasing levels of unemployment? Take technological and legislative changes and developments into consideration as well. Does computerization exert an influence at all upon your market? Are new laws being passed which could have knock-on effects in any way?

Having built up a broad-based awareness of the marketplace over your years of trading, you ought to be able to draw yet more conclusions about the validity of radio advertising in this instance. Knowing that many key players in the industry regularly tune in to a specific feature – perhaps a weekly 'What's on' guide, a sports round-up or the network chart show – might persuade you to promote yourself on this radio station and at that particular time. Being aware that radio is soon to encompass regional stations for the first time which succinctly cover your entire marketplace may encourage you to consider the medium more fully than before, when it was local and highly fragmented by nature. Refer to 'Viewing the market: an action checklist' on page 29. This will help you with your planning.

FIRMS	GOODS AND SERVICES	ADVERTISING ACTIVITIES	RADIO
Features:	Features:	Stations:	Characteristics:
		Timings:	
Positive:	Strengths:	Frequency:	Advantages:
		Lengths:	
Negative:	Weaknesses:	Contents:	Disadvantages:
		Duration:	

Thinking about your rivals: an action checklist

Filling in the gaps

You should be able to answer almost all of your questions about customers, rival firms and the market from your own existing knowledge and by checking records and chatting informally with selected individuals. You certainly should have enough information to conclude whether radio is or is not a fitting advertising medium for your business at this given time. Nevertheless, you ought to try to discover the answers to *all* of your queries if you intend to press ahead to advertise over the airwaves, and wish to be as successful as possible. Your notes – about the business, goods and services, targets, customers, competitors and the marketplace – will prove to be invaluable when you have to draft a schedule, compose advertisements, and so on.

Locally, radio stations often commission and/or conduct surveys and make their findings available to prospective advertisers (see Appendix A: Independent radio stations, page 85). You might also obtain help and additional information from Chambers of Commerce and local authorities, many of which publish statistical reports of potential interest to you. The Association of British Chambers of Commerce can supply appropriate addresses. Refer to Appendix D: 'Useful contacts', page 140. Various surveys, statistics and reports may be stocked in your local library, and it is worth talking to a librarian to see what is available there, and if it is relevant to you.

Radio bodies, advertising organizations and your own professional or trade association can be of significant assistance, telling you more about customers, competitors and the marketplace, as and where necessary. The *Directory of British Associations* outlines more than 6,500 trade bodies in the United Kingdom, and should be available at your nearest library. Alternatively, contact the publisher, CBD Research Limited. The government and its numerous departments – especially the Department of Trade and Industry – produce innumerable guides, reports and statistics which are sold through Her Majesty's Stationery Office. Some may be of significance to you. See Appendix D: 'Useful contacts', page 140. Find out all you can by approaching anyone and everyone who may fill in the gaps in some way.

Summary

1. Potential radio advertisers should analyse their customers, rivals and the marketplace, carrying out additional research as and when necessary. This analysis will allow them to:
   a) conclude whether radio is a suitable or unsuitable advertising medium for them;

THE MARKET

1. Size

2. Turnover

3. Organization

4. Administration

5. Representative associations

6. Regulatory bodies

7. Other organizations

THE INFLUENCES

1. Political

2. Economic

3. Social

4. Demographic

5. Technological

6. Legislative

7. Other influences

RADIO

Characteristics:

Pros:

Cons:

Viewing the market: an action checklist

b) accumulate information and detailed notes of use during a subsequent radio advertising campaign, if appropriate.

2. Analysing customers involves various tasks:
   a) creating a picture of the 'typical' customer – whether a business or an individual;
   b) finding out as much as possible about their thoughts, opinions and radio listening habits;
   c) considering the relevance of radio in relation to the customer base.

3. Competitors need to be appraised too. In particular:
   a) their key features, goods, services, strengths and weaknesses;
   b) their past and present radio advertising activities, if appropriate;
   c) the value of radio as an advertising medium for them, and other, would-be advertisers.

4. Assessing the marketplace means:
   a) understanding its size, make-up and activities;
   b) contemplating the numerous influences upon it, and their possible effects;
   c) calculating the validity of radio advertising in such a situation.

5. Most prospective radio advertisers will be able to access information about their customers, rivals and marketplace with relative ease. Additional data may be obtained from a variety of sources including:
   a) local radio stations, business associations, authorities and libraries;
   b) radio bodies, advertising organizations and professional associations;
   c) the government, especially the Department of Trade and Industry.

5 Fixing an appropriation

NOW THAT YOU ARE CONVERSANT with the radio world, regard it as a potentially viable medium in your individual circumstances, and possess extensive and detailed notes for future use, you can consider how much to spend on your forthcoming advertising activities. Naturally, it is hard to decide what is the 'right' sum of money to set aside for advertising over the next quarter, six months or year, especially if you are a first-time advertiser (and harder still to make final decisions on the ways in which to spend it). Analysing sales, appraising profits and contemplating other influential factors will help you to allocate a suitable budget – or 'appropriation' – for your radio advertising campaign.

Analysing sales

Start off by thinking carefully about your turnover last year. Many successful advertisers base their advertising budget upon a percentage of their previous sales figures, typically in the region of 1 to 5 per cent. Clearly, there is some merit in advertising in line with known sales, although significant drawbacks can also be associated with this method. It is difficult to settle upon a fitting percentage, whether 1, 3, 5 per cent or whatever. Also, a low turnover last year means a smaller appropriation is set for this year, when more money may be needed for advertising to help to boost sales. Similarly, a high turnover in the preceding year inevitably leads to a larger budget being allocated this time around when it might not be so necessary. It is easy to under- or overspend with this backward-looking approach.

Contemplate your current sales levels. There is some support for fixing an appropriation in relation to a percentage of existing turnover, week by week or month to month. Spending a proportion of what is currently being received might be thought to be sensible and thrifty, and more up-to-date than basing it on last year's, long-gone performance. Nevertheless, the problem of choosing an appropriate percentage still remains. In addition, it may be a shortsighted policy to adopt since this week's or month's figures may be especially good or bad and bear no relation to what you actually want to achieve in the next month, quarter or year. It is a head down – almost in the sand – attitude.

Calculate and consider your anticipated turnover for the forthcoming quarter, six-month period or year, with a view to establishing a budget linked to a percentage of that total, estimated figure. Visibly, this is a forward-looking approach relating advertising to what you want to happen in the future, instead of what has already occurred in the often dim and distant past. Once again, selecting a relevant percentage is tricky. So too is predicting exactly what your sales are likely to be in an upcoming period of time, given the rapidly changing and developing nature of the marketplace these days. You may find that you under- or overestimate turnover, leading to an equally inappropriate advertising budget.

Work out the cost price of your 'average' product and/or service, breaking it down into this much for raw materials, that much for labour and so forth, and incorporate advertising within your calculations. Aiming to sell so many units in a given period, you can simply multiply the individual advertising cost by the appropriate number of units to be sold to derive the advertising budget for that specific time span. This is another approach which looks ahead and associates advertising with what you want to achieve and is therefore of some value. However, it is really only of short-term use and needs to be constantly monitored and amended, since internal costings may increase or decrease and external influences can have noticeable, knock-on effects as well.

Appraising profits

Check out the profits that you made during your last trading period. Some advertisers decide to tie their advertising appropriation to a percentage of their profits instead of their sales turnover. Obviously, there is much to be said for spending only what you can afford to pay out and no more, especially for a small firm operating in troubled, recessionary times. Nevertheless, key criticisms exist. Yet again, it is not easy for you to settle upon the right percentage to spend. Furthermore, substantial remaining profits suggests that more money will be allocated to advertising activities when it may not be required, and vice versa. You need to be careful to avoid the endless, downward spiral of reduced profits, less advertising, lower sales, smaller profits and so on.

Keep an eye on the profits which are being generated by your business on an ongoing basis per week, and each month. You may wish to set aside and pay out a certain proportion of these monies on your advertising for the next, matching period. Maintaining a close watch upon your income and expenditure on a step-by-step basis so that you do not spend more than is coming in is a wise policy for any firm to adopt, whether large or small. Knowing the exact amount to put to one side remains an enigma though, and such an approach also smacks of little more than a survival policy, etching out a day-to-day living and no more. This is acceptable for hand-to-mouth businesses, but others may prefer to look ahead, spotting challenges and opportunities, and advertising to take advantage of these, which is difficult to do if this month's profit is minimal and you only have a few pounds put by to promote yourself.

Try to ascertain what your profits may be for a given period in the future, perhaps for the forthcoming quarter, six or twelve months. Think about setting an appropriation that is related to a percentage of the anticipated sum. Clearly, this is a much more dynamic and forward-thinking stance to adopt, rather than looking backwards all of the time. As always, it is hard to fix a percentage that is suitable in the circumstances and it is even harder to calculate what your profits are likely to be over a specific time. Such a far-sighted approach will have to be nurtured carefully, one step after another to see that your business remains on course, with amendments made as and when necessary.

Taking the sales price of your 'typical' product and/or service, divide it up into this amount for costs, and that amount for profit. Mindful of the profit, you can then attribute a certain percentage of it to advertising, usually between 5 and 10 per cent as you see fit. Multiplying this amount by the number of units you expect to sell provides you with a potential advertising budget for that period. Forward-looking though it may be, you will almost certainly have costed it all out on the basis of today's individual mix of figures which will inevitably shift and alter as time goes by, leaving you to have to continually update your calculations.

Contemplating other factors

Of course, there are various, alternative ways of setting an advertising appropriation rather than relating it to sales and/or profits of the past, present or future. You may budget by tradition whereby the same sum is spent on advertising each year, with allowances made for increased costs, inflation and so forth. From hands-on experience, you are aware of the response generated by a given quantity (and specific mix) of advertising and are happy with that. For businesses operating in certain, static circumstances – such as the sole trader beavering away in a workshop only able to take on one job at a time – this method may well be quite satisfactory. Most other concerns trading amid ever-developing scenarios will conclude that it is inflexible: too high in some instances and too low in others.

Another popular technique is to base your advertising budget around those of your competitors, on the rough and ready principle that if you spend the same sums you will acquire a similar market share, and by spending more will increase it accordingly. Clearly, it is sensible to be broadly aware of what other firms allocate to their promotional activities, especially if you are advertising for the first time, or are entering a new and unfamiliar marketplace. Everything being equal, you would expect your budget to be in approximate proportion with their budgets, as appropriate. Nevertheless, it is extremely hard to spot each one of your rivals' advertisements and therefore to calculate their total appropriations. Also, all businesses are distinctive in terms of size, goods, services, goals and so on, so any comparisons need to take careful account of the differences that exist between competing concerns.

An increasingly used and relevant method of establishing an appropriation is to simply set out short-, medium- and long-term objectives – to generate 1,000 enquiries, produce £10,000 sales or whatever – and then calculate how much advertising needs to be carried out to achieve these targets. Working back from the total numbers and types of advertisements, for example, a relevant budget can be set. In its favour, this approach does look ahead, trying to match advertising expenditure to future goals. However, it takes skill and hard-won experience to work out the advertising levels required to meet the objectives and it is easy to spend endless sums to make certain of success.

Allocating a suitable budget

To finalize a fitting appropriation, you ought to reflect upon the various approaches one after the other, separating them out into relevant and irrelevant methods, so far as you are concerned. For example, if you are the owner of a new concern, you obviously cannot base your budget upon past sales, profit or tradition, but can consider linking it to present and future sales and profits, competitors' appropriations and your upcoming goals. Taking the potentially suitable techniques in sequence, assess the advertising budgets which would be derived from each of them. This will leave you with a range of figures which is often surprisingly close, below which would probably be insufficient, and above which might be excessive for your needs.

With minimum and maximum figures in mind for your appropriation, you should then refer to those notes that were built up during your preliminary work and research, and which will now begin to prove their worth to you. Consider all aspects of your firm, and its influence upon your budget. For example, if it is well sited with plenty of passing trade you may feel you need to spend less on advertising than if it were located in the back of beyond. Think about your products and services. As an example, launching a new range of innovative goods will clearly necessitate more extensive advertising than simply reminding customers about well-established products. Contemplate those goals again if you have not already taken account of them in ascertaining your range of figures.

Similarly, spend some time mulling over your customers and what you know about them. For example, advertising your concern, goods and services to a group of clients in one compact area is likely to be far less costly than trying to promote yourself to a large number of customers based here, there and everywhere. Review your competitors once more if you did not assess them when you were piecing together your range of top-to-bottom budget figures. Also consider the marketplace in which you trade or plan to operate within in the near future, mindful of its effects upon your advertising appropriation. If you are trying to break into a new market, you may feel that you need to spend more on advertising than if you were attempting to expand in your existing marketplace, where you are better known.

After contemplating the different approaches and your individual situation, you will be able to settle upon an approximate budget which seems to be suitable for your needs. Whatever the figure is that you have in mind, it ought to be flexible, capable of being raised or lowered by an appropriate amount to allow for changing circumstances. You must be ready to review sales, profits, competitors' activities and so forth as you go along, adjusting your levels of advertising expenditure as necessary to meet challenges and grasp opportunities that open themselves up to you. Be prepared to drop below or go above your minimum and maximum figures, if a developing situation suggests this is the appropriate course of action to take. To assist you, 'Allocating a suitable budget: an action checklist' can be completed. It is on page 36.

Summary

1. Deciding how much to spend on radio advertising is a hard task but may be made easier by:
   a) analysing sales;
   b) appraising profits;
   c) contemplating other factors;
   d) allocating a suitable budget based on these activities.

2. An advertising appropriation may be set with regard to:
   a) past sales;
   b) present sales;
   c) future sales;
   d) the cost of goods and/or services sold.

3. Alternatively, it could be linked to:
   a) past profits;
   b) current profits;

Method	Relevance/irrelevance	Minimum/maximum sum	Budget figure
1. % past sales			
2. % present sales			
3. % future sales			
4. % cost price			
5. % past profits			
6. % present profits			
7. % future profits			
8. % selling price			
9. By tradition			
10. By comparison			
11. By target			

Allocating a suitable budget: an action checklist

c) future profits;

d) the profit of goods and/or services sold.

4. Some radio advertisers set an appropriation in relation to:

a) tradition;

b) competitors' activities and perceived budgets;

c) short-, medium- and long-term objectives.

5. A suitable budget may be allocated by:

a) reflecting upon the alternative approaches, and selecting the most relevant ones in the circumstances;

b) calculating 'minimum' and 'maximum' figures to spend;

c) taking account of the accumulated notes compiled earlier about the firm, goods, services, goals, customers, competitors and marketplace;

d) settling on an approximate sum which is used in a flexible manner.

6 Planning your activities

HAVING COMPLETED the groundwork and established an appropriate budget for your advertising activities, you can begin to approach radio stations, peruse rate cards, assess audiences and calculate costs before preparing your schedule for your radio advertising campaign. It is at this point that all of your careful and occasionally tedious preparatory work really begins to pay dividends, with those copious notes helping you to make the correct choices about various aspects of your approaching campaign.

Approaching radio stations

Initially, it is important to obtain a full and complete list of commercial radio stations in the United Kingdom. Appendix A: 'Independent radio stations', page 85, provides key details. However, new stations are transmitting all the time so it may be advisable to update this information by referring to *British Rate and Data* – or BRAD as it is more often known – which is a 600-page, monthly publication published by Maclean Hunter Limited, detailing various media. Data about radio stations includes broadcasting frequencies, addresses, telephone numbers and contact names, audience figures, advertising rates and trading terms and conditions. Check it out in your local library rather than buying it as a one-off purchase or by annual subscription, both of which are costly. See Appendix E: 'Recommended reading', page 142.

It should be a relatively straightforward task to reduce this comprehensive list to a short-list, simply by referring to your back-up notes, as and where necessary. If you own a small business seeking to sell to nearby customers only, you need to make a note of the handful of stations that broadcast in your area. Similarly, should you be aiming to expand distribution and sales into surrounding areas or across a region or the whole country, you should write down the details of those radio stations that transmit over the relevant places. When you have worked through each radio station on the original, lengthy list, you may find that you are left with perhaps three to six stations which are worth contacting.

You can then write to or telephone one station after another, asking them to forward information to you, as a prospective advertiser. At this stage, avoid arranging to meet any sales executives, as is often suggested, since you really need to analyse the radio stations and what they can do for you as an advertising medium, prior to discussing your advertising, negotiating terms and ordering your first package of advertisements. If you are thinking of using several stations and subsequently find it easier to book all your advertising through one central source, you may prefer to approach the relevant sales house(s), whether Independent Radio Sales, Media Sales and Marketing, the Radio Sales Company or whoever. *British Rate and Data* gives guidance on which sales houses act for the various stations. Refer to Chapter 2: 'Who's who in radio', page 8 and Appendix D: 'Useful contacts', page 140.

Perusing rate cards

Each radio station and/or sales house approached should send a rate card (or cards) to you, on request. Within these glossy pamphlets, you will discover key facts about its broadcast area or transmission area, probably with a map showing how far afield the station can be heard and the population in that region, perhaps broken down demographically by sex, age and social grade. Alongside this, there should be details about the total audience reached, divided up demographically into sexes, ages and social grades, and in their thousands and percentage terms too. Average, half-hourly audience figures may also be given, highlighting how these increase and decrease through the day and week. Hopefully, these data will have been independently audited.

Advertising rates will be set out per thirty-second spots – and for other ten-, twenty-, forty-, fifty-, sixty-second spots – at different times of the day. Various segments will be identified – perhaps 6 a.m. to noon, noon to 6 p.m., 6 p.m. to midnight and midnight to 6 a.m. – with rates established according to listening figures during those times. Details of surcharges and discounts offered will be explained, albeit under a variety of names. Not surprisingly, surcharges will apply at peak listening times earlier in the day and later in the week, whereas discounts are applicable at quieter times towards the end of the day and at the beginning of the week. Surcharges or 'fixing charges' as they are also popularly known, are added if you wish your advertisements to be transmitted during specific periods or in special positions, perhaps between 9 a.m. and 11 a.m. or after news breaks instead of being run out evenly across the station's schedule.

Discounts crop up in many guises on the rate card. 'Volume', 'contract' or 'expenditure' discounts are extremely commonplace and are made available if you guarantee to spend a certain sum with the station over a given period. Advertisements will be re-invoiced at the higher rate at the end of that time if you fail to spend the agreed amount. 'Advance booking' discounts, or 'incentives', may apply to orders placed perhaps a month or so ahead of transmission.

'Combination' discounts exist if your advertisements are broadcast over two transmission areas, which happens when a radio station has split frequencies, broadcasting over AM and FM wavebands. 'First time' or 'test market', discounts could be on offer too, for advertisers using this medium on an initial, trial basis.

The basic terms and conditions involved with buying a package of advertisements will be spelled out in the rate card. In particular, airtime is generally booked according to the availability level in force at the time the booking is taken. Obviously, only a limited amount of advertising airtime is available and is usually offered on a first-come, first-served basis. If you book late, you will not only pay a higher rate, but will find the best spots have already been allocated elsewhere. All new customers will be expected to pay for their advertising in advance, perhaps seven days or more ahead of transmission. Advertisements may be cancelled without charge if written notice is received by the station at least twenty-eight days prior to being broadcast. A sliding scale of charges will apply thereafter – perhaps 10 per cent of the bill for fourteen working days written notice, 20 per cent for seven working days and 40 per cent for three working days.

Brief details may also be provided about the production of advertisements, which are invariably put together by the radio station on behalf of its advertisers, especially small businesses which simply do not possess the in-house resources and expertise required to produce quality advertisements themselves. The cost of a basic commercial consisting of one voice with one piece of music or a sound effect will be stated. Data about additional voices, music, sound effects and copies of the advertisements made available to you on cassette will be noted as well. See Chapter 7: 'Composing advertisements', page 58.

Other miscellaneous information will be incorporated within the rate card. Facts and figures may be supplied about the station's history, programme schedules and presenters, music and associated services, and overall aims. The advantages of radio advertising could be promoted heavily along with details of major advertisers who have used the radio station, and their opinions of it. See the rate card for what it is – sales literature containing a mix of data and sales hype which is exaggerated as far as possible to make you want to spend money with that particular station. You need to recognize this, and be able to sort out the relevant details – audience figures, advertising rates, terms and conditions, production facilities – from the less important sales blurb. Peruse the rate cards on pages 41 to 48 to distinguish the key details from the sales hype, which will help you later on when you really have to do it. Then take a look at 'Perusing rate cards: an action checklist' on page 49.

Figure 6.1: Rate Card

Profile

Radio Trent began broadcasting from its historic Georgian building in the heart of Nottingham in July 1975 and quickly established itself as a radio station in tune with the City and County. In October 1988 it became one of the first radio stations in Britain to create two separate twenty four hour a day programme outputs with TRENT-FM and GEM-AM.

The station has won many awards including the coveted Sony Award for Programming and twice, the equally prestigious award for Locally Made commercials. The station has always been at the forefront of development in the radio industry. Innovative programming and technical developments have contributed to Radio Trent's success and high reputation amongst professional broadcasters and listeners alike.

Trent runs the industry's only full-time Training School. The Radio Training Unit trains broadcasters, engineers and journalists. The school is also becoming increasingly involved in business courses for the public and private sector. Recent clients have included Texaco, British Telecom, Boots, Local Authorities and the DSS.

Radio Trent's programming is designed to appeal to a wide cross section of listeners throughout the diverse and dynamic transmission area stretching from Mansfield and the mining communities of North Nottinghamshire to the rich

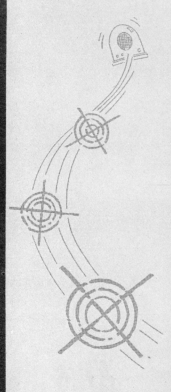

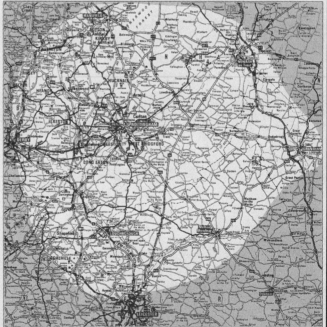

agricultural areas of Grantham and the Vale of Belvoir, from historic Newark on Trent in the East to the Erewash Valley in the West. It is an area which includes a wide range of industries, many of which have common household names, including Boots, Raleigh, Pedigree Pet Foods, Plessey, Wrangler and Speedo.

The programming reflects this buoyant and confident area with a wide range of music, comprehensive news and sports coverage, and special programmes focussing on business, the arts and fashion. TRENT-FM and GEM-AM with their individual sound and style complement each other perfectly, winning an ever increasing audience.

Rate Card

LOCAL ADVERTISING RATES

Figures represent £'s Sterling

SEGMENTS		60 SEC	50 SEC	40 SEC	30 SEC	20 SEC	10 SEC
P1	0600-0900 MON-FRI 0900-1200 SAT-SUN	202	185	146	112	90	56
P2	0900-1200 MON-FRI 0600-0900 SAT-SUN	171	157	124	95	76	48
P3	1200-1500 MON-SUN	97	89	70	54	43	27
P4	1500-1800 MON-SUN	104	96	75	58	46	29
P5	1800-2400 MON-SUN	41	38	30	23	18	12

DAYTIME PACKAGE MON-SUN 0600-1800						
SPOT LENGTH	60 SEC	50 SEC	40 SEC	30 SEC	20 SEC	10 SEC
COST	144	132	104	80	64	40

TOTAL AUDIENCE PACKAGE MON-SUN 0000-2400hrs						
SPOT LENGTH	60 SEC	50 SEC	40 SEC	30 SEC	20 SEC	10 SEC
COST	106	97	77	59	47	30

NIGHT TIME PACKAGE 35 SPOTS MON-SUN 2400-0600hrs						
SPOT LENGTH	60 SEC	50 SEC	40 SEC	30 SEC	20 SEC	10 SEC
COST	270	248	195	150	120	75

RATINGS PACKAGE COST £1090				
	ADULTS	MEN	HWIVES	19-34 ADULTS
UNIVERSE (000)	1090	531	525	411
TOTAL HOURS	6897	3837	3040	2232

AMOUNT OF EXPENDITURE REQUIRED	DISCOUNT
£10,000+	10%
£15,000+	15%
£20,000+	20%
£30,000+	25%
£40,000+	30%

LOCAL ADVERTISING RATES
Are only available to companies whose businesses are predominantly confined to the Trent-FM and GEM-AM broadcast area.

ACCOUNTS
Accounts shall normally be paid not later than seven clear working days before scheduled broadcast date unless by prior agreement. When an agreement has been reached, accounts must be paid within 28 days of the date of invoice. The existence of a query on an individual item on an account will not affect the due date of payment of the balance.

CASH WITH ORDER DISCOUNT
A discount of 5% will be made available for payments at the same time as an order is placed. This discount only applies to air-time orders placed by account customers and is not a pre-payment discount.

PRODUCTION AND RECORDING FACILITIES
A fully equipped studio and an experienced creative team are available to produce commercials tailored to specific needs. Prices on request.

FIXED SPOTS
Subject to availability, advertisers may fix their basic rate spots at a surcharge of 10%.

CANCELLATION PERIOD
Air time is cancellable by either party provided that notice is received 28 days prior to the scheduled broadcast date. In the event of a cancellation, the advertiser will be charged at the appropriate rate to the number of commercials broadcast or scheduled to be broadcast within that period

TRENT·FM **96·2** NOTTINGHAM GEM·AM **999** NOTTINGHAM

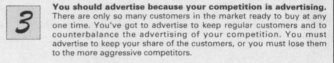

Advertising
WITH US...THE REASONS WHY

1 **You should advertise to make more sales.** Advertising works. Businesses which succeed are usually strong, steady advertisers. Look around. You'll find the most aggressive and consistent advertisers are almost invariably the most successful.

2 **You should advertise continuously.** Shoppers don't have the store loyalty they once had. Cars give shoppers mobility and freedom. You must advertise to keep pace with your competition. An international retail body has stated that: "Mobility and non-loyalty are rampant. Stores must promote to get former customers to return, and to seek new ones."

3 **You should advertise because your competition is advertising.** There are only so many customers in the market ready to buy at any one time. You've got to advertise to keep regular customers and to counterbalance the advertising of your competition. You must advertise to keep your share of the customers, or you must lose them to the more aggressive competitors.

4 **You should advertise because there is always business to generate.** Your doors are open. Salespeople are on the payroll. Even the slowest days produce sales. As long as you're in business, you have overheads to meet and new people to reach. Advertising can generate customers now...and in the future.

5 **You should advertise to reach new customers.** Your market changes constantly. New families in the area mean new customers to reach. People earn more money, which means changes in lifestyles and buying habits. The shopper who wouldn't consider your business a few years ago may be a prime customer now. Remember...Families will move this year... People will be married... Babies will be born.

6 **You should advertise because it pays off over a long period.** Advertising gives you a long term advantage over competitors who cut back or cancel advertising. A five-year survey of more than 3,000 companies found:
Advertisers who maintain or expand advertising over a five-year period saw their sales increase an average of 100%.
Companies which cut advertising averaged sales increases of 45%.

7 **You should advertise to keep a healthy positive image.** In a competitive market, rumours and bad news travel fast. Advertising corrects misleading gossip and "overstated" bad news. Advertising that is vigorous and positive can bring shoppers into the marketplace, regardless of the economy.

8 **You should advertise to generate store traffic.** Continuous store traffic is the very first step towards sales increases and expanding your base of shoppers. The more people who come into the store, the more possibilities you have to make sales and sell additional merchandise. For every 100 items that shoppers plan to buy, they make 30 unanticipated "in-the-store purchases."

9 **You should advertise to remain with shoppers through the buying process.** Many people postpone buying decisions. They often go from store to store comparing prices, quality and service. Advertising must reach them steadily through the entire decision-making process. Your name must be fresh in their minds when they ultimately decide to buy.

10 **You should advertise to maintain store morale.** When advertising and promotion are suddenly cut or cancelled, sales people may become alarmed and demoralised. They may start false rumours in an honest belief that your business is in trouble. Positive advertising boosts morale. It gives your staff strong additional support. Advertising boosts the confidence of shareholders.

ADVERTISING ■ ADVERTISING ■ ADVERTISING ■ ADVERTISING

Audience

	UNIVERSE '000s	WEEKLY REACH '000s	%	TOTAL HOURS '000s	AVERAGE HOURS
ALL ADULTS 15+	1080	556	51	6237	11.2
ADULTS IN HOME	1080	431	40	4026	9.3
MEN - ALL	526	287	54	3322	11.6
15-34	204	122	60	1365	11.2
35+	322	164	57	1956	11.9
WOMEN - ALL	554	296	49	2915	10.8
15-34	201	103	51	781	7.6
35+	353	166	47	2134	12.9
AGE 15-24	215	128	60	689	5.4
25-34	190	97	51	1458	15.0
35-54	335	194	58	2688	13.8
55+	340	136	40	1402	10.3
HOUSEWIVES - ALL	537	256	48	2834	11.1
WITH CHILD	175	87	50	904	10.4
SOCIAL CLASS					
ABC1	399	188	47	1076	5.7
C2DE	681	367	54	5161	14.0
CHILDREN					
5-14	170	72	40	440	6.1

WEEKLY REACH

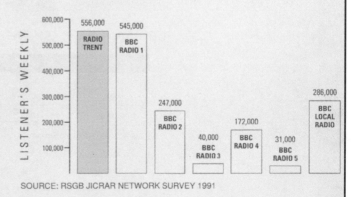

SOURCE: RSGB JICRAR NETWORK SURVEY 1991

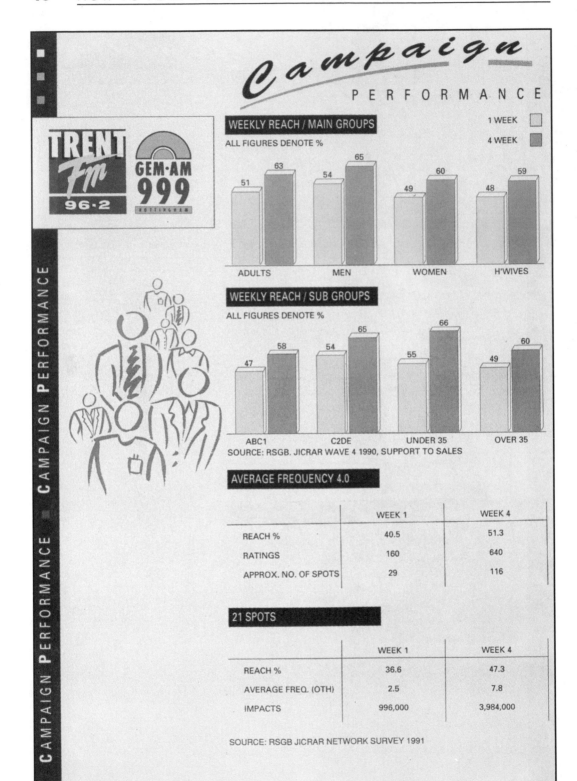

Campaign PERFORMANCE

WEEKLY REACH / MAIN GROUPS

ALL FIGURES DENOTE %

| | 1 WEEK |
| | 4 WEEK |

	ADULTS	MEN	WOMEN	H'WIVES
1 WEEK	51	54	49	48
4 WEEK	63	65	60	59

WEEKLY REACH / SUB GROUPS

ALL FIGURES DENOTE %

	ABC1	C2DE	UNDER 35	OVER 35
1 WEEK	47	54	55	49
4 WEEK	58	65	66	60

SOURCE: RSGB. JICRAR WAVE 4 1990, SUPPORT TO SALES

AVERAGE FREQUENCY 4.0

	WEEK 1	WEEK 4
REACH %	40.5	51.3
RATINGS	160	640
APPROX. NO. OF SPOTS	29	116

21 SPOTS

	WEEK 1	WEEK 4
REACH %	36.6	47.3
AVERAGE FREQ. (OTH)	2.5	7.8
IMPACTS	996,000	3,984,000

SOURCE: RSGB JICRAR NETWORK SURVEY 1991

Programme
S C H E D U L E S

Broadcasting contemporary hit music, album tracks and great oldies with hourly news and weather, and frequent local information, keeping you in touch 24 hours a day.

MON/FRI

06.00-09.30 Gary Burton
with The Breakfast Show

09.30-13.00 Rob Wagstaff
with The Morning Show

13.00-14.00 The Music Jam
- Continuous Hit Music

14.00-18.00 Andy Miller
with The Afternoon Show

18.00-20.00 **Monday: The Eurochart** - Europe's
favourites with Pat Sharpe.
**Tuesday: The Trent FM weekly Top Thirty with
Gary Burton** - A second chance to hear
Nottinghamshire's most popular singles.
Wednesday: Electric Wednesday with Craig Strong.
**Thursday: 18.00-18.45: The Business Programme
with Ann Marie Minhall** - Weekly update of news and
discussion for Nottinghamshire's business community.
18.45-19.00: The Look with Louise Moore - Fashion
Programme.
19.00-20.00: The Break - Neil Fox talks to the music
headliners.
Friday: America's Choice - Benny Brown with the
American Top Forty.

20.00-00.00 Mon / Thurs: Tim Disney
with The Late Show
Friday: Phil McKenzie with The Late Show

00.00-01.00 Midnight Love Affair with Viv Evans
- Music for Late Night Lovers

01.00-03.00 Greatest Songs
with Viv Evans

03.00-06.00 The Early Show
with Mark Burrows

SATURDAY

06.00-09.00 Danny Cox
with The Breakfast Show

09.00-12.00 Tim Disney
with The Morning Show

12.00-15.00 Andy Miller
with The Lunchtime Show

15.00-18.00 Craig Strong
with The Afternoon Show

18.00-22.00 Phil McKenzie

22.00-01.00 Get on the Good Foot with
Mark Spivey - Playing the Latest
Dance Music

01.00-06.00 Greatest Songs
with Graham Wright

SUNDAY

06.00-09.00 Tim Disney
with The Breakfast Show

09.00-12.00 Rob Wagstaff
with The Morning Show

12.00-14.00 The Trent FM weekly Top Thirty
with Gary Burton - unveiling
Nottinghamshire's most popular singles

14.00-16.00 Craig Strong
with The Afternoon Show

16.00-19.00 The Network Chart -
David Jensen counts down the
Nations Top Thirty

19.00-20.00 The Break
with Neil Fox

20.00-00.00 Adrian Air

00.00-01.00 Midnight Love Affair with Viv Evans
- Music for late night lovers.

01.00-06.00 Greatest Songs
with Viv Evans

News and Weather on the hour 24 hours a day

Trent FM's Careline broadcasts throughout the day
Monday to Friday.

P R O G R A M M E ■ S C H E D U L E S

SCHEDULES

Solid gold radio playing the hits of the past four decades with hourly news and weather, keeping you in touch 24 hours a day.

GEM·AM
EAST MIDLANDS

MON/FRI

06.00-10.00	The John Peters Breakfast Show
10.00-13.00	The Tony Lyman Morning Show
13.00-13.10	Report at One
13.10-14.00	Goldmine - Continuous hit music.
14.00-18.00	The Afternoon Show with Andy Marriott - (Including Report at Five)
18.00-21.00	The Golden Juke Box with Brian Tansley
21.00-00.00	Late Night Gem with Steve Voce
00.00-01.00	Midnight Love Affair with Viv Evans - Music for late night lovers.
01.00-03.00	Viv Evans with Music for the Early Hours
03.00-06.00	Mark Burrows with Music for the Early Hours

(In the Leicester area on the **1260kHz AM** frequency the following programme may be heard between 18.00 and 22.00. SABRAS - programming for Asian listeners)

SATURDAY

06.00-10.00	The Breakfast Show with Paul Robey
10.00-14.00	The Morning Show with Steve Voce
14.00-18.00	Music and Sport with Neil Metcalf

LEICESTER ONLY
14.00-15.00 This week in history: Les Ross
15.00-17.00 David Hamiltons Music Show
17.00-18.00 Sportstalk

18.00-19.00	Alternatives, The East Midlands Arts Magazine with John Shaw
19.00-22.00	Saturday Night Gold with Viv Evans
22.00-01.00	The Hidden Gem with John Shaw
01.00-06.00	Graham Wright with Music for the Early Hours

SUNDAY

06.00-09.00	The Breakfast Show with Andy Marriott and Richard Steel
09.00-12.00	Sunday Requests with Tony Lyman
12.00-14.00	Double Hit Parade with John Peters - Featuring two top ten's from years gone by.
14.00-17.00	The Afternoon Show with Brian Tansley.
17.00-19.00	Saviles Travels with Jimmy Savile
19.00-22.00	Sounds Country with Tim Rogers
22.00-00.00	Late Night Sunday with Richard Steel and Martin Mitchell
00.00-01.00	Gem Goldmine with Viv Evans
01.00-06.00	Graham Wright with Music for the Early Hours

(On Sunday we offer a choice of listening on **945kHz** 19.00-22.00 Apne Sangeet with Amerjeet and Raj - programming for Asian listeners)

To ensure that you have studied each rate card properly, you should ask yourself whether or not you have read about the following points. You ought to be able to say 'Yes' to every question.

	Yes	No
The transmission area	❑	❑
Population, numbers and types	❑	❑
Audience, numbers and types	❑	❑
Half-hourly audience figures	❑	❑
Advertising rates	❑	❑
Advertising segments	❑	❑
Surcharges	❑	❑
Discounts	❑	❑
Terms and conditions	❑	❑
Production facilities	❑	❑
Miscellaneous data	❑	❑

Perusing rate cards: an action checklist

Assessing audiences

Your first consideration when studying the key information on the rate cards must be to compare and contrast each station's audience alongside your own targeted one. Do not be concerned about the breadth of a radio station's transmission area, nor the total numbers and types of people which it can potentially be heard by. Hyped up though these superficially impressive facts may be by the rate card and most especially by the station's employees, they are almost wholly irrelevant to you. However wide a territory is covered and whoever has the chance to tune in, it does not necessarily mean that those people in the area will listen any more than everyone who has an opportunity to buy a newspaper, visit an exhibition or go to the cinema actually does.

Pay closer attention to the radio station's weekly reach, in terms of numbers and types. These figures should be independently audited either by Radio Joint Audience Research or a reputable research company such as National Opinion Polls so that you can feel confident that they have been calculated in an honest and straightforward manner. Even so, do be very aware that the figures quoted are only estimates based on limited samples, and findings for the same stations have in the past been at odds with each other which suggests discrepancies exist somewhere. Also, and of equal significance, these figures may be up to a year or so old. Bear in mind that this is a rapidly developing industry in which new radio stations are being launched regularly, taking away listeners from older, established stations.

Taking the material that you have (which despite its flaws is still likely to possess a broad, albeit rather loose, semblance of accuracy), write out each radio station's audience, broken down in numbers and types by sex, age, social grade and so forth. From your notes, set out your own (prospective) customer base in the same manner. Taking sex, age and so on at a time, compare their make-ups – or 'profiles' – together, section by section to see how far each division and the overall groups match or differ from the other. Obviously, you are looking to retain those stations whose audiences resemble your own as closely as possible. There is little or no sense, for example, in advertising to a predominantly male audience if your customers are mostly female, to young listeners when you wish to reach older ones.

Similarly, ascertain how far each radio station's audience penetrates into your customer base, again evaluating and comparing one at a time and section by section. For example, perhaps you are trying to promote your business, products and services to the 100,000 young people between 15 and 24 years in a region and can see that one station reaches 25,000 or 25 per cent of them whereas another reaches 50,000 or 50 per cent and so on. Likewise, you are attempting to appeal to an ABC1 audience which totals 200,000 in number and a radio station reaches 100,000 or 50 per cent of them whilst the next reaches 120,000 or 60 per cent. Clearly, you can then rank remaining stations into an order of preference on those grounds. See 'Assessing audiences: an action checklist' on page 52 for more help in this area.

Calculating costs

Having shortened and prioritized your list of radio stations on the basis of how many and who they reach, you should then set about calculating and comparing the costs of advertising yourself and your goods and services via each of these stations. This is not an easy task given the range of packages on offer, the diversity of rates, surcharges and discounts available and the different numbers and types of people who tune in to the respective radio stations. Nonetheless, it is worthwhile making some comparisons, however approximate they may be, in order to identify those stations which look as though they will be the most cost-effective for your firm.

The traditional way of making value-for-money comparisons between media is to work out the cost of reaching every 1,000 people within each medium's audience. For radio stations, you might take the cost of a standard thirty-second spot – free of surcharges, discounts and the like – and divide it by one thousandth of the weekly reach to obtain a 'cost per thousand figure'. For example, one station charges £50 for thirty seconds and has an audience of 200,000. Thus, £50 is divided by 200 (200,000 ÷ 1,000) which equals 25 pence. Another radio station charges £80 per thirty-second spot and possesses an audience of 350,000. Hence, £80 is divided by 350 (350,000 ÷ 1,000) which represents 23 pence, and so on.

Naturally, you are well aware that although this method of evaluating media alongside each other is sound, it is inappropriate to simply compare and contrast each radio station's total audience – as some naive advertisers do – since these do not precisely match your own audience in terms of types and numbers. Superficially, the station with a 23 pence figure seems to be better value than the other at 25 pence, but perhaps the first radio station's audience resembles your own more closely. If that first station charges £50 and reaches 50,000 of your audience and the second charges £80 and contacts 75,000, then the first represents better value, at £1 per thousand compared to £1.07 per thousand.

Again, you must also be very conscious that you will not be buying one, thirty-second spot on its own, but will be purchasing a package of advertisements. Some will be shorter at twenty seconds, others longer at forty seconds. Some will be broadcast in the morning, others in the afternoon. You may have your advertisements rotated evenly through the schedule, or transmitted at

STATION'S AUDIENCE

1. Numbers

2. Sexes

3. Ages

4. Social grades

5. Location

6. Other characteristics

TARGET AUDIENCE

1. Numbers

2. Sexes

3. Ages

4. Social grades

5. Location

6. Other characteristics

Assessing audiences: an action checklist

specific times. Your campaign of 28, 112 advertisements or whatever could last for a week or a month or more. All radio stations have different pricing structures to reflect these many and varied alternatives so it is wise to keep recalculating and recomparing costs as far as you can, seeing which station is most cost-effective for twenty- and forty-second advertisements, morning and afternoon broadcasts and so on, until you are wholly confident of your conclusions.

Preparing your schedule

Having concluded which stations to use because they seem most likely to reach the right numbers and types of your targeted audience at the right price, you then need to go on to piece together a preliminary schedule of radio advertisements. Initially, you must decide exactly when you should promote your goods and services – which time of the day, what part of the week, which month, what quarter and so on. Your gut reaction, which will be the same as many other first-time radio advertisers, is to choose those times of the day, week and so forth that attract the most listeners, whether between 6 a.m. and 9 a.m., Thursdays and Fridays rather than Mondays and Tuesdays, or whatever. This is unwise as these times may not necessarily be best in *your* circumstances.

The timing of your advertisements must derive from your own unique situation, as personified in your notes on your business, products, services and goals, those concerning your customers, competitors and the budget available to you. Base your decisions on them, and them alone. Your firm may open from 5 p.m. until midnight so it might not be appropriate to advertise in the mornings when customers cannot immediately telephone or visit you in response to your advertisements. Goods and services may be seasonal, which could suggest certain weeks or months to you. It would be more sensible to promote romantic gifts in the week before Valentine's Day than the week after, and school uniforms in August before the new academic year rather than in October. Your goal might be to increase sales in spring instead of autumn, summer rather than winter.

All of the background research which provided you with these notes may have informed you that your existing and would-be customers listen to the chosen radio station in the mornings instead of the afternoons, during weekdays rather than at weekends. Successful, national rivals might promote themselves in fixed months or quarters, giving you a lead which you may be wise to follow. Aware of imminent political changes or legislation that might adversely affect your marketplace, you could decide to advertise sooner rather than later. Your budget may restrict you to advertising at less instead of more expensive times.

Then, you need to work out how long your advertisements should be, whether ten, twenty, thirty, forty, fifty, sixty seconds or even longer. Although thirty seconds is the norm and the length quoted in most rate cards, it should not be an automatic choice. Again, you ought to reach a decision suited to your own circumstances. You may prefer longer, more detailed advertisements to give status to your business, to explain the main functions of your goods and to achieve your objective of maintaining a high profile. You could select shorter advertisements because your customers are busy people and your budget is limited. You will need to take account of creative considerations too, when making a choice. See Chapter 7: 'Composing advertisements', page 58.

Moving on, you should consider how often you ought to advertise – whether every hour or other hour, day after day or alternate days, twenty-eight times in a week, a fortnight or whatever. Go through your accumulated notes once again, to enable you to decide. A new concern usually needs to be promoted more often than an established one if it is to become as well known. Seasonal goods ought to be advertised rapidly before they are unavailable. Regularly used services should be promoted steadily to remind customers of their many benefits just before the next purchase is made or order placed. Your goal might be to boost sales which points to more frequent advertising, not less, and so on.

Similarly, you have to contemplate how long your advertising campaign ought to last, whether for a short, sharp month or a slow and steady quarter. Perhaps your customer base is constantly changing and evolving, with new people coming into the marketplace and others leaving. This might suggest an ongoing, steady level of advertising. Possibly a new rival is opening, and a short burst of rapid, quick-fire advertising at and around that time may be fitting. Of course, the market in which you operate could have trading peaks and troughs which might indicate advertising times and durations to you.

Aware of the most appropriate timing, length and frequency of your advertisements and the duration of your planned activities, you can draft out a proposed schedule for your radio advertising campaign. Make a note of the stations you intend to use, the number of advertisements to be transmitted for each one, their lengths, preferred dates and times, the costs incorporating surcharges and discounts and the total, estimated expenditure which ought to fall somewhere between your minimum and maximum, budget figures. You are then ready to translate this possible schedule into practice, composing advertisements and getting in touch with radio stations and/or sales houses to conduct your campaign. The 'Media schedule' form on page 55 may be of use to you at this stage.

MEDIA SCHEDULE

Campaign: _____ Number: _____

Medium: _____ Date: _____

Medium / Week beginning												

Media schedule form

Summary

1. The build-up to advertising on the radio should be tackled on a step-by-step basis. It involves:
   a) approaching radio stations;
   b) perusing rate cards;
   c) assessing audiences;
   d) calculating costs;
   e) preparing a schedule.

2. When approaching radio stations, it is sensible to:
   a) obtain a complete list and details of commercial radio stations in the United Kingdom;
   b) draw up a short-list of 'possibles', by referring to these details and the accumulated notes about the firm, goods, services, goals, customers, competitors and the marketplace;
   c) contact selected radio stations for rate cards either directly or via a central source such as a sales house.

3. Rate cards should be perused with particular regard to the stations':
   a) transmission areas;
   b) audiences;
   c) advertising rates, discounts and surcharges;
   d) terms and conditions of advertising;
   e) production facilities;
   f) other facts and figures provided.

4. Radio stations' audiences must be compared alongside the target audience. This means:
   a) studying each station's weekly reach, in terms of numbers and types;
   b) analysing them in relation to the main features of the target audience;
   c) appraising how far each station's audience penetrates into the target audience.

5. When calculating the costs of advertising on the different radio stations, it is advisable to:
   a) work out the cost of reaching 1,000 of each station's audience with a thirty-second advertisement;
   b) re-calculate costs with regard to the numbers and types of the target audience reached;

c) re-calculate costs in relation to the numbers and types of advertisement used.

6. A schedule should be prepared which specifies:
   a) the chosen radio stations;
   b) the timing of advertisements;
   c) the length of advertisements;
   d) the frequency of advertisements;
   e) the duration of the campaign.

7 Composing advertisements

YOU NOW NEED to think about your advertisements, selecting your approach, choosing their contents and making sure that they comply with the law and are thus acceptable to the radio stations and the listening public. Realistically, you will leave the actual creation and production of the advertisements to the stations' production teams. As a small-business owner or manager, you simply do not have the in-house skills and expertise needed to plan and record advertisements which are good enough to be transmitted on air. Nevertheless, you will have various thoughts and ideas that you can put in writing or on tape for submission to the radio stations to ensure they produce the advertisements that you want.

Selecting your approach

Various approaches may be taken towards radio advertisements, and humour is probably the most popular. A funny situation, catchphrase or jingle, voices, music or sound effects can capture the listeners' attention, so that they hear the advertisements and what you are trying to say to them. Handled properly, humour may be very effective and can leave a lasting impression. However, it is hard to be truly funny. An idea which seems hilarious to you now may be less so to the listener struggling out of bed bleary-eyed at 6 a.m. in the morning. Your in-house jokes and silly voices – side-splittingly funny though they may be to colleagues – could appear nonsensical to the outside world. Sometimes, really humorous advertisements can detract from your message. The catchphrase or jingle is recalled, instead of the concern, products or services. The 'Cracker' radio script on page 59 shows an example of a funny *and* successful radio advertisement.

You could seek to appeal to listeners' emotions, using a mix of different voices, music and sound effects to play upon their maternal or paternal instincts, desire for status, nostalgia for times gone by, or whatever. These may attract and retain the listeners' interest, helping them to absorb your message. For example, a gentle caring voice, soothing music and the sound of a baby gurgling in the background may be attractive to young mothers who would then

'Cracker'

SFX:	(Cracker being pulled, rustling of paper)
MVO: (without emotion)	Doctor, doctor, I feel like a pair of curtains. Pull yourself together man.
SFX:	(Cracker pulled)
	What shakes on the sea bed? A nervous wreck.
SFX: (authoritative)	(Cracker pulled)
	What animal is it best to be on a cold day? A little otter.
	(Sigh)
MVO:	If you want something a little more stimulating to read this Christmas, the bumper edition of 'The Economist' is out tomorrow/out now.

'Cracker' radio script

'Mr Dobie'

Mr Dobie:	My name's Paul Dobie, and this is what happened to me last March.
	I was feeling sick whilst driving along the M6 and decided to pull on to the hard shoulder in my Volvo Estate.
	After a short while I felt better, and put my safety belt on to continue my journey.
	But it wasn't just nausea that hit me that day.
	I looked in the mirror and to my horror saw a lorry speeding towards me on the hard shoulder.
	I was hit from behind with incredible force. My Volvo was spun around, tipped onto its side, and pushed 200 yards up the motorway into a ditch.
	I climbed out of the car and discovered I'd been struck by a 40-ton articulated lorry with a JCB Earth Mover on the back.
	I reckon if it hadn't been for the Volvo's passenger safety cell I'd never have known what hit me.
MVO:	Volvo. A car you can believe in.

'Mr Dobie' radio script

'Box'

Miranda Richardson: Famous Names liqueur chocolates come in a box.

They have no sugary layer which makes them deliciously smooth.

At Christmas I asked my husband Nigel to buy me some Famous Names liqueur chocolates.

Nigel bought me a tin of scented talcum powder.

SFX: Gun-shot.

Now Nigel comes in a box.

Deliciously smooth Famous Names liqueur chocolates.

The perfect present for discerning palates.

'Box' radio script

'Wind'

SFX:	Irish country music throughout.
Donald Sutherland:	It was a Friday evening and Joe found himself on the way to the bar. He also found his brother Michael with him, and his friend Eddie. Joe and Michael but not forgetting Eddie turned the corner and the wind fair sandpapered their cheeks.
SFX:	(music)
	'Why,' thought Joe 'was this enjoyable?' Was it perhaps because if he felt his eyes watering and his ears burning cold he must be alive? Or maybe it was because he liked the wind. It was so . . . bracing! Or was it simply because there was a glass of Beamish with his name written on it that would soon be slipping and sliding down, in the lovely warm bar?
SFX:	(music)
	'Answer C' thought Joe, who had always been so good at multiple choice.
SFX:	(music)
MVO: (sensual)	Beamish Stout. Just slips away.

'Wind' radio script

listen to what you were telling them. Alternatively, you might adopt a more logical approach, winning over listeners with sensible, reasoned arguments. As an example, a firm but friendly voice may spell out the key selling points of a new, executive car to convince businessmen and women that it is worth buying. Look at the 'Mr Dobie' radio script on page 60 to see how this advertisement plays on listeners' emotions.

Using a well-known personality to praise your firm, products and services on air is another, increasingly popular technique, which can give status and credibility. When that person is seen or heard again elsewhere on television or radio, listeners may be reminded of your products once more. Of course, it is important that he or she is perceived to have the same qualities – honesty, reliability, integrity and the like – that your business has and also possesses an appropriate and instantly recognizable voice. Bear in mind that employing a personality is costly, often running into hundreds or even thousands of pounds for just a few hours' work. It can be risky too, if he or she becomes involved with other activities which may be racier than the image you want to convey, or is mixed up in a scandal. The 'Box' radio script on page 61 and the 'Wind' radio script on page 62 were read by Miranda Richardson and Donald Sutherland respectively. In both cases, the personalities were considered to have played a key role in the success of the advertisements.

Bullish small-business owners and managers advertising on the radio can sometimes be drawn into a comparative approach, comparing and contrasting their firms, goods and services with those of their rivals. Typically, the prices of their products are quoted and direct or indirect, knocking references are then made about the prices of competitors' goods. This may seem to be a sensible and successful approach, especially if you are genuinely better than your rivals in some respects. Nonetheless, it is a dangerous attitude to adopt. You are drawing the listeners' attention to your competitors, and giving them free advertising time. Knocking rivals is also regarded as being in poor taste and a sign that you are worried about your competitors. Customers may visit them to see why you are so concerned, and buy from them. Also, you have to be absolutely sure of your facts, to avoid legal action being taken against you by outraged rivals.

Whatever your favoured approach – and you will probably have some ideas of your own on the subject – always be mindful of the particular benefits and drawbacks of this highly individual medium. For example, the radio is live and immediate, with advertisements being recorded and transmitted very quickly if necessary. Price cuts could therefore be notified to existing and would-be customers within a few hours. Similarly, this is a localized medium, so a humorous and well-known local incident might be referred to in an amusing and topical manner. See Chapter 1: 'Types of radio', page 1, to refresh your memory of the advantages of radio advertising.

Do not overlook the drawbacks of radio though. As an example, it is one-dimensional, with advertisers dependent upon sound only. You cannot show the products you are trying to sell, their colours and varieties and so on, and are unable to demonstrate them. You need to conjure up the required image by voices, music and sound effects alone. You may find it hard to make listeners feel nostalgic for your products and services simply by describing them. It is a shortlived medium too, with advertisements lasting for seconds rather than minutes. It is difficult to work through reasoned arguments in such a limited period of time. Refer to Chapter 1: 'Types of radio', page 1, to remind yourself of the disadvantages of advertising on air.

Not surprisingly, your selected approach must also reflect your specific situation. Humour may be appropriate for a joke shop, but not for a funeral parlour. Playing on listeners' emotions could be relevant for baby goods, but less so if financial services are being offered. Obtaining an endorsement from a popular personality may be more suited to a large, national firm than a small business operating on a restricted budget. Comparing yourself with competitors might just be worth considering if you are that much better than them in *all* respects, but not if you are closely matched. Work through your background notes to finally conclude which approach is right for you. See Chapter 3: 'Evaluating your business', page 15 and Chapter 4: 'Understanding the marketplace', page 23.

Choosing contents

Aware of the type of approach that is correct for the medium *and* your particular circumstances, you then have to decide upon your sales message. Be clear about what you want to say, and why you wish to state it. Perhaps you want to stress the enormous numbers and types of products stocked by your shop, in order to attract customers and boost sales. Possibly, you wish to outline a job vacancy to appeal to suitable applicants and to enable you to pick the right person. Whatever your aim and reasons are, be fully familiar with them prior to writing down or recording any of your ideas. Each voice and every statement, piece of music and sound effect used must be chosen with these in mind.

Start advertisements by immediately trying to seize the listeners' attention and to make them tune in to what you are about to tell them. A clear and commanding voice may achieve this, as could a funny, cartoon-like one or an instantly recognized voice, perhaps quoting a famous catchphrase. Soft and sentimental music, a rousing burst of song or a well-known, much-loved jingle might be equally effective. Sound effects – as diverse as an opening door or the rat-tat-tat of gunfire – could be used too, in order to draw the listeners into your world. Whatever you pick – and there are hundreds and thousands of voices, snatches of music and sound effects to choose from at a radio station – attempt to separate the listeners from the last song or advertisement in a definite manner, to turn their attention onto your advertisement. Take another look at the 'Cracker' radio script on page 59 to see how this advertisement begins.

Sketch out the main part of your advertisements by noting down your sales message and the points that you wish to put across to substantiate and enhance it, whether the name of your shop and a list of the main types of goods stocked or details of your firm, the job and the person required to fill it. Keep your notes as simple as you can. Bear in mind that you are advertising via an unseen medium, and for only thirty seconds or so. Elaborate descriptions and endlessly repeated points will not convey and support your message – they will just confuse and obscure it. Make sure that your points are brief and wholly relevant, and are sorted into a sensible order. The 'Mr Dobie' radio script on page 60 is a good example of this.

Contemplate the type of voice which should be used to put over your message. For example, a breathless one speaking quicker and quicker as he or she tries to mention all of your products in time might be both humorous *and* effective, especially if topped and tailed with a contrasting, cool and rather amused voice reminding listeners of the name and address of your well-stocked shop. Similarly, a kind but authoritative voice could be most appropriate for a logically approached recruitment advertisement, informing job hunters of the reasons why they should apply for this vacancy and encouraging them to do so. Should you want to have two characters chatting, perhaps about your first-class products, try to see these people in your mind, giving them names, personalities and a reason for the conversation. This will help you to write a real dialogue, and enable the stations to interpret your wishes more accurately. See the 'Box' radio script on page 61. Miranda Richardson's voice is just perfect for this advertisement.

Think about the background music and sound effects that might be added to your advertisements to support your key points. As an example, fast and furious music could be played alongside that quick-speaking voice to underline the vast range of goods that need to be referred to within the thirty seconds or so, and to make it sound even funnier. For the job advertisement, the noise of a busy office, full of dynamic people going about their tasks, might be fitting, making would-be applicants want to work there. Do not be afraid of silence though. It is not always relevant to fill your advertisements with music and sound effects. A clear, well-spoken voice putting across your points may be sufficient, and could stand out from the hurly-burly of the loud advertisements around it. The Irish music and soft, warm voice of Donald Sutherland combine to great effect in the advertisement on page 62, 'Wind'.

End advertisements by attempting to inspire the listeners to act, whether to pick up the telephone and place an order with you or to jump into their cars and drive to your shop. Having stated the reasons why they should buy from you, apply for the job or whatever, make them feel that they must do something *now*, perhaps by indicating that stocks are limited, a sale will end soon or that there is a closing date for job applications. Then help them to respond by reminding them of your firm's name, telling them where you are and what your telephone number is. Give them a contact name as well, if appropriate. Close off the advertisements by repeating the opening piece of music, sound effect or whatever, to separate them from the following ones. Check out how the radio advertisement on page 59, 'Cracker' ends – it's very effective!

Do write down all of your thoughts and ideas about your advertisements so that they can be passed to the production departments of the radio stations. Better still, tape an advertisement, doing the voice yourself and adding music and sound effects if you are able to. This may make you feel self-conscious, but it is worthwhile. Playing back the tape, you can judge the voice, the message, music and sound effects for yourself, deciding if they are all suitable. You may conclude that thirty seconds is not long enough to put over your message, or perhaps you are trying to convey too many points. However amateurish it may sound, it will also be of great help to the production teams, enabling them to produce what you want to hear, and at the first attempt.

Complying with the law

It is important that your advertisements comply with the Radio Authority's Code of Advertising Standards and Practice (and Programme Sponsorship). This Code applies to all advertisements transmitted on radio stations licensed by the Authority, and contains a number of over-riding principles. Radio advertising must be legal, decent, honest and truthful. Advertisements have to adhere to the law in every respect. Advertising rules referred to in the Code should be applied in spirit as well as by the letter. The Code is divided into three parts. Section A covers the standards for the presentation of advertisements. Section B deals with the contents of advertisements and is followed by appendices looking at key categories of some concern to the Authority. Section C considers programme sponsorship, which is less relevant to you.

You need to be aware of the rules and guidelines concerning the presentation of your advertisements, as set out within Section A of the Code. In particular, advertisements must be clearly distinguishable from programming. For example, you should avoid using sound effects associated with news bulletins which could cause confusion. Various types of advertisement must not be broadcast during certain programmes. Typically, advertisements for contraceptives or sanitary protection products are not to be transmitted in or around children's programmes. Advertisements for some products and services must not be broadcast at all. As examples, cigarettes, pornography and escort agencies cannot be promoted on air. Station presenters must not endorse or recommend advertisers' goods. Therefore, you could not employ these personalities to praise your products. Other, less significant rules are that radio stations must not discriminate for or against any advertisers, and product placements within programmes are prohibited.

Of course, the contents of advertisements are of equal concern, and you should thus be familiar with the rules and guidelines noted in Section B of the Code. Of key relevance, advertisements must not mislead. For example, you should not state that a product will restore hair growth, if it does not. Advertisements must not offend against good taste or decency, or be offensive to public feeling. Typically, you should not use profane language or make unkind references to minority groups. Advertisements must not unfairly attack or discredit other products. As an example, competitors' goods should not be described using a denigratory tone of voice. Advertisements must not use sound effects likely to create a safety hazard to drivers. It would therefore be unwise to incorporate the sounds of sirens or screeching tyres within your advertisements.

Some advertising receives special attention from the Radio Authority and its Code incorporates appendices containing additional, detailed rules and guidelines on such advertisements. These appendices cover the do's and don't's of financial advertising, alcoholic drink advertising, children and advertising, medicines, treatments and health, charity advertising, environmental claims and religious advertising. If your advertisements fall into any of these categories, it is absolutely essential that you not only study and understand Sections A and B of the Code but also read the appropriate appendix carefully. Section C of the Code relating to the sponsorship of programmes need not be looked at, unless and until this becomes an area of interest to you.

Sensible though it is that you are wholly conversant with the Code and its relevant sections, radio stations will act as a censor if you unintentionally breach the rules or guidelines. They are authorized by the Radio Authority to approve or reject most advertisements, although others such as those involving financial services, alcohol and so on are referred to the Association of Independent Radio Companies Limited for clearance prior to transmission. If in doubt, approach the radio stations, AIRC or the Radio Authority itself for advice and guidance. See Chapter 2: 'Who's who in radio', page 8, and Appendix C: 'Code of Advertising Standards and Practice', page 117.

8 Running your campaign

HAVING ADOPTED an extremely thorough, step-by-step approach towards this particular medium, you should be more than capable of running a winning advertising campaign over the airwaves. Your careful and conscientious build-up will have given you both the knowledge *and* the confidence to go on to purchase airtime, conduct a trial run in order to assess your initial activities, and amend your schedule in a way which puts you in a position to mount a successful campaign. You have what it takes to be a winner.

Purchasing airtime

With your proposed schedule and advertisement notes to hand, you can telephone the radio stations (or sales houses) in turn to talk to and arrange to meet their sales executives. Some of these go-betweens are good at their work, others less so. Some know the radio world inside out, understand their station and what it has to offer advertisers and will recognize your needs and try to fulfil them to your satisfaction. They are a mine of valuable information and hands-on assistance. Others seem to be employed only for their looks and are capable of doing little more than smiling sweetly and writing down your order. Nevertheless, you do need to meet sales executives as you cannot expect to post your schedule and advertising ideas to the station in the hope that someone correctly interprets your requirements.

Usually, a sales executive will call on you at your shop, office or factory within a day or so of your telephone conversation. It is a good idea to encourage the exchange of views and opinions during a chat over tea or coffee. Establish a rapport, if you can. Talk generally about radio advertising and its pros and cons. Perhaps the executive will tell you something you do not know or may stress an advantage or disadvantage you have not thought about thoroughly. Discuss who's who at the station so that you are aware of who will be doing what for you. Chat about radio bodies and advertising organizations too, perhaps updating your knowledge of RAJAR's role and findings in the industry.

Talk over your small business, your goods and services, goals, customers, rivals and the marketplace. Clarify your thoughts if necessary, and see whether the sales executive has any valid comments or suggestions to make. Outline the budget that you have allocated to your radio advertising activities, the minimum and maximum amounts, and what you feel able to spend via the radio station. Discuss your proposed schedule and the timing, length, frequency and duration of your advertisements, and the reasons behind your choices. Find out if the executive agrees with them. Explain your advertisement ideas, and why you believe this approach and these contents are right for your firm. Hear what the sales executive has to say about them.

Of course this valuable, two-way exchange may not be possible if you are faced with an executive who simply agrees with everything you say because he or she just wants to sell you as much airtime as possible. Even so, you will both still need to cover your proposed schedule in some depth, thrashing out the prospective number of advertisements allocated to the particular station, their respective lengths and possible dates and times, whether rotated evenly at the radio station's discretion or planned for specific periods or special breaks. Clearly, you have to discuss your wishes and see what is available before reaching agreement on the numbers and types of advertisements to be scheduled.

Again, you will both have to discuss your advertisement thoughts in some considerable detail. You need to outline the approach that you think is most suitable for your firm, products and services. The planned contents of your advertisements have to be talked through as well, with you explaining what it is you want to say to your customers and describing the types of voices, music and sound effects that are required to put over your message in the most effective manner. Once more, you have to ascertain whether – and if so, how far – your ideas can be translated into reality by the radio station.

It is very tempting to book your entire schedule at once, perhaps to take advantage of the discounts stated in the rate card or even to impress the sales executive, as some foolish small-business owners and managers seek to do. This is wholly unwise, and at odds with the steady and measured build-up which you have adopted to date. Do no more than book an initial batch of advertisements – possibly for the first week, fortnight or month at most – with the remaining ones being pencilled in for subsequent confirmation, adjustment or cancellation, as appropriate. You need to be able to appraise various aspects of your schedule and advertisements – timing, frequency, duration and so forth – and measure their effects before settling upon or amending your plans as necessary.

Having discussed your schedule and advertisements together, you then have to finalize the costs and any other terms and conditions associated with the booking. Always push for discounts, whether first time, payment in cash or bulk discounts, on the basis of what you intend to spend with the station over the coming year. Never forget that the radio world is growing rapidly and more and more stations are competing to attract the same number of advertisers in the marketplace, so take advantage of this as far as you can. Whatever the costs indicated on the rate card, tough bargaining should ensure these are reduced by between 10 and 25 per cent.

Make sure other terms and conditions are worked through and understood by both parties at this stage to avoid confusion and disagreements later on. The rate card will already have stated the basic terms and conditions which advertisers are deemed to have accepted upon placing an order. You may wish to try to have these varied or added to, when relevant. In particular, do insist that the executive arranges to supply you with a copy of the advertisements produced for you by the station, well before they are due to be transmitted. You must be able to check and approve these in advance. Also, avoid paying up front. You have to be absolutely happy with the advertisements and satisfied with the station's performance before handing over your money. Make this an unbreakable rule.

Following your meeting with the sales executive, confirm your agreement in writing, sending it to him or her at the radio station. Do this in good time, and well before your advertisements are due to be produced and transmitted on air. Set out the numbers, lengths, dates and times of your first advertisements. Write down the agreed approach to, and contents of, your advertisements, including an accompanying cassette containing your prepared example. Note the costs, discounts and other terms and conditions that were negotiated between you. Remind him or her to pencil in subsequent advertisements to be decided upon, one way or the other. Keep a copy of your letter, in case the original goes astray.

If necessary, chase up the executive thereafter to obtain copies of the advertisements which have been prepared on your behalf by the station's production team. Check that your thoughts and ideas have been interpreted correctly, and the approach and contents are what you wanted. Make certain the voices, music and sound effects are how you imagined them to be, and put over your message in as effective a manner as possible. Listen for errors such as a mispronounced name, an incorrect dialling code or an incomplete telephone number, which can and do crop up surprisingly often. Do not hesitate to demand changes as and when necessary. Your reputation and money are at risk if you do not.

Conducting a trial run

You must view your initial batch of advertisements as a trial run, and an opportunity to test your schedule and advertisements, measure the responses and adjust your plans if this seems sensible. You have to try to discover if you are advertising via the right radio stations. It is important to find out whether you are promoting yourself at the best times and as frequently and for as long as you ought to do. You need to learn if the approach to and contents of your advertisements are correct, and are as successful as they could be. In short, you must feel sure – or at least as certain as you can be – that you are on the right lines, before you go further with your campaign.

Attempt to hear all of your advertisements as they are transmitted – which may not be an easy task if you have booked perhaps twenty-eight advertisements to be spread out over one week. Nevertheless, the more you listen to, the better. You ought to make your own preliminary judgements of your schedule and advertisements, and can only do this by tuning in. Check to see that advertisements were broadcast at the agreed times, if appropriate. If timings were left to the radio station, see that they were transmitted at relevant times for your particular target audience. As an example, those which are broadcast in the early hours of the morning may be wasted if your audience comprises housewives with young children.

On hearing your advertisements as they are transmitted, decide for yourself whether they really are the right length. Imagine that you are the targeted customer, and calculate if you would be able to absorb the message in such a short time; or possibly the advertisements now seem to be too long, seeking to put across too much information to the audience. Advertisements always sound different when they are played on air. Contemplate the frequency of your advertisements, working out to your own satisfaction whether they are well spaced out, too close together or too far apart. It is not unknown for advertisements which are supposed to be rotated evenly over one week to be grouped on one or two days at the end of that period.

Think about the advertisements themselves in more detail. Hearing them again over the airwaves, you may feel that the overall approach is rather low-key or too upbeat for your specific message. The contents could be too brief or overly detailed. You may believe that the voices, music and sound effects do not convey your message in the appropriate manner. Check to ensure that any changes you had demanded – from an incorrectly quoted telephone number to quieter sound effects – were implemented. Be sure the advertisements were transmitted in full, and that the beginnings and ends were not cut off or talked over as sometimes happens. Listen to what else is broadcast around your advertisements. Quite rightly, you could feel that advertisements from rival firms may detract from yours. Similarly, a discussion about mad cow disease may not be the best time to promote your meat pies, sausages and related foodstuffs.

Do not hesitate to contact the radio station if you are unhappy with any aspect of your schedule or advertisements, whether timings, lengths, frequency or whatever. If the station is at fault – transmitting advertisements at inappropriate times, leaving notified errors uncorrected, presenters chatting over your advertisements and so on – then it should remedy the matter immediately and be prepared to adjust your subsequent invoice accordingly. Should you have changed your mind, perhaps about the length of the advertisements, the voices, music, sound effects and so forth, it is not too late to make changes. Never forget that radio is an instant medium, and advertisements can be re-recorded in hours and broadcast within minutes.

In addition to your own judgements concerning your schedule and advertisements, it is wise to try to assess your customers' responses to them so that you can see which times, lengths and other factors generate the best results. In theory, you can spot which advertisements initiated responses by including an identifying element – or 'key' into each and every advertisement transmitted. Listeners may be asked to telephone a specific person, write to a different address or quote a particular reference number when placing an order, buying a product or applying for a job. For example, recruitment advertisements in the mornings could ask listeners to telephone Alan Smith, with those in the afternoons calling Jenny Taylor. Thus, responses can be recorded, attributed to advertisements and conclusions drawn.

However, this method is difficult to operate in practice via the radio except on a very limited basis such as comparing and contrasting the success rates of advertisements broadcast in the mornings and afternoons, weekdays and weekends. Trying to evaluate many variable factors alongside each other becomes impossible as innumerable versions of the same advertisement have to be produced with Alan Smith quoted for morning advertisements, Jenny Taylor for afternoons, Tom Reynolds for twenty-second advertisements, Jane King for forty-second advertisements and so on. This is time-consuming and costly to do and, even then, there is no guarantee that listeners responding to the advertisements will mention the specific name.

It is more sensible to talk to as many customers who enquire about, place orders for or buy your goods and services as possible. Ask them whether they heard your advertisements, which ones, what they thought of them and if these advertisements inspired them to call, write to or visit you. As a small-business owner or manager dealing with a relatively limited number of customers on a day-to-day basis, you ought to be able to speak to them all and draw conclusions from their various comments and suggestions.

If enquiries, orders and sales are not always channelled through you, it may be harder still to assess responses to your schedule and advertisements. You could need to ask sales representatives to act for you, posing questions to the customers on your behalf. Should your goods be sold through numerous outlets, you may have to content yourself with conducting audits of opening stock levels, deliveries and closing stock levels and comparing figures with previous periods whilst making allowances for changing circumstances. This will at least allow you to conclude that radio advertising has had an overall, worthwhile effect, or not.

Make a point of reading through the invoices that are subsequently sent to you by the radio stations or delivered by the sales executives. Mistakes are commonplace, so do be sure that they are correct, with the right numbers and types of advertisements listed, discounts given and so forth, before handing over your money. Often, the invoices will be brought to you by the executives who will want to know your opinions of the advertising to date, and whether you wish to take or cancel the other advertisements which have been pencilled in. You then have to decide whether your radio advertising has been successful or not. Hopefully, it will have been, and you will want to carry on, albeit with some amendments to your trial activities. 'Conducting a trial run: an action checklist' on page 76, and the 'Media assessment' form on page 77 may enable you to reach valid conclusions.

Amending your schedule

Conscious of your personal views and the responses of your customers towards your schedule and advertisements, you can then set about making amendments to them, as and where necessary. You may decide to reduce or increase the number of radio stations you use, if it seems that your target audience is excessively or inadequately covered. You might concentrate on one station rather than another from now on if one is noticeably more successful than the other. It may be apparent that advertising in the mornings produces significantly better responses than in the afternoons, so you can thus adjust your schedule as a consequence of this. You could feel that your advertisements need to be lengthened to have a greater impact upon your existing and would-be customers.

It may be wise to add to or to cut back upon the number of advertisements that are being transmitted over the airwaves, so the target audience hears them enough times to absorb your message but not so much that they become bored, and ignore what you are saying to them. Similarly, you could decide to close up or widen the gaps between each advertisement transmitted. You might conclude that the approach and/or contents of your advertisements to date need to

When conducting a trial run, it is sensible to assess advertisements personally in the first instance. Ask yourself if the following points are satisfactory or not. Hopefully, all your answers will be 'Satisfactory".

	Satisfactory	Unsatisfactory
Timings	❑	❑
Lengths	❑	❑
Frequency	❑	❑
Approach	❑	❑
Contents	❑	❑
Preceding advertisements	❑	❑
Subsequent advertisements	❑	❑
Programmes	❑	❑

Conducting a trial run: an action checklist

MEDIA ASSESSMENT FORM

Campaign:

Number:

Medium:

Date:

Medium	Cost incurred (£)	Number of enquiries	Cost per enquiry (£)	Number of orders	Cost per order (£)	Total sales	Average sale per enquiry (£)	Average sale per order (£)	Comment

Completed by:

Signature:

Checked by:

Signature:

Media assessment form

be amended for the future, perhaps replacing a strident voice which irritated your customers and prospects with a softer one, and changing music or sound effects accordingly.

However minor or major your amendments may be, it is essential that you proceed with your advertising activities in a slow and careful manner. Book no more than one month's advertisements at a time, analysing them and the responses as you go along and prior to booking any more. Do bear in mind that your judgements to date are based upon short-lived knowledge and experience, and simply may not be valid: only time will tell. Similarly, responses have been derived from a limited number of advertisements and probably are sufficient enough for you to conclude that radio advertising has been worthwhile, but no more than that. Detailed and accurate assessments about timings, lengths, frequency and so on, build up over a lengthy period of time.

Furthermore, circumstances change as months and quarters pass by, necessitating further amendments to schedules and advertisements. The radio industry will continue to expand throughout the 1990s, with increasing numbers of stations transmitting across the United Kingdom on a local, regional and national basis. You will have more choice, which may be reflected in your upcoming schedules. The Radio Authority's Code of Advertising Standards and Practice will be updated further to meet developing situations, and might influence what you advertise and how you promote your goods and services much more than it does at the moment. Radio Joint Audience Research figures may differ dramatically from one year to the next – often diminishing and affecting your selection of those radio stations which will be given your advertising.

Your small business might expand into new trading areas, leading you to promote yourself via regional or national rather than local radio stations. You may diversify into other products and services, with the approach to and contents of your advertisements affected as a consequence of these developments. Your objectives could shift and alter over a period of time with similar adjustments being made to your advertising patterns. Customer habits might change, with people tuning in to more diverse stations catering for increasingly specialized needs. Rival firms may promote themselves on one station but not another, thus affecting your plans. Anything can happen, and you must adopt an ongoing, hands-on approach to your radio advertising activities if you are to become – and remain – a winner.

Summary

1. Those radio advertisers who have planned carefully are most likely to run a successful campaign. To ensure this, they need to:
   a) purchase airtime effectively;
   b) conduct a trial run;
   c) amend their schedule, if appropriate.

2. Purchasing airtime should be approached on a step-by-step basis. It involves:
   a) contacting radio stations to arrange to see their sales executives;
   b) meeting sales executives to exchange knowledge, thoughts and ideas;
   c) booking an initial batch of advertisements;
   d) finalizing costs, terms and conditions;
   e) confirming everything in writing;
   f) checking everything is being done satisfactorily, and on time.

3. It is essential that a trial run is conducted. This allows:
   a) the schedule and advertisements to be tested;
   b) responses to be measured, and assessed;
   c) plans to be adjusted, if relevant.

4. Conducting a trial run properly means:
   a) listening to the advertisements, and appraising them objectively;
   b) discussing shortcomings with the radio station if necessary;
   c) measuring responses, so far as possible;
   d) talking to customers, and seeking their opinions;
   e) studying invoices to make certain they are correct, and querying errors.

5. Following a trial run, a schedule will often need to be amended, with regard to:
   a) radio stations used;
   b) the timing of advertisements;
   c) the lengths of advertisements;
   d) the frequency of advertisements;
   e) the duration of the campaign.

6. Radio advertising should be tackled in a slow and careful manner, because:
   a) it takes time to make detailed and accurate assessments about schedules, advertisements, success or failure;
   b) the industry is constantly changing, and offering new choices and alternatives;
   c) businesses, goods, services, objectives, customers, rivals and the marketplace are evolving all the time too.

Conclusion: the radio advertiser's checklist

YOUR FIRST advertising activities on the radio ought to be successful and, if they are, you will probably decide to promote yourself via this medium time and time again. Before going on, do look back at what you have done so far, reviewing each stage in turn so that you can recognize your successes and failures. You should be able to answer all the following questions in a positive manner. If any of your responses are negative, this will indicate that improvements can be made to forthcoming campaigns.

Types of radio

❑ Did you learn about the characteristics of radio stations across the United Kingdom?

❑ Were you fully familiar with the advantages of advertising on air?

❑ Were you wholly aware of the disadvantages of advertising over the airwaves?

❑ Did you compare and contrast these characteristics, pros and cons with regard to your own situation?

Who's who in radio

❑ Did you find out about the departments and employees within a radio station, and what each of them do?

❑ Were you conversant with the trade bodies in the radio industry and their respective roles?

❑ Were you conscious of the professional organizations in the advertising world and their activities?

❏   Did you ask these various bodies for information and guidance as and when appropriate?

Evaluating your business

❏   Did you look at your concern and its mix of positive and negative features?

❏   Did you study your goods and services, spotting their particular pluses and minuses?

❏   Were you able to clarify your targets in the short, medium and long term?

❏   Were detailed notes taken for use during your campaign?

Understanding the marketplace

❏   Did you consider your customers, finding out as much as possible about them?

❏   Did you think about your rivals, identifying their strengths and weaknesses?

❏   Did you view the market and discover the influences upon it?

❏   Were you able to fill in the gaps in your knowledge by conducting further research, as required?

❏   Were in-depth notes prepared for use with your advertising activities?

Fixing an appropriation

❏   Did you analyse your sales in the past, during the present and for the future?

❏   Did you appraise your profits for previous, current and forthcoming years?

❑   Did you contemplate other influential factors before setting your appropriation?

❑   Was a suitable budget allocated for your radio advertising campaign?

Planning your activities

❑   Did you approach radio stations after composing a shortlist on the grounds of where you wanted to promote yourself?

❑   Did you peruse rate cards, separating key information about audiences, advertising rates and conditions from out-and-out sales hype?

❑   Did you assess each radio station's audience in relation to your own targeted audience?

❑   Did you calculate costs on a 'cost per thousand' basis, making as many detailed, value-for-money judgements as possible?

❑   Did you prepare a schedule of advertisements which was right for your unique circumstances?

Composing advertisements

❑   Did you select the best approach for your advertisements on this occasion?

❑   Did you choose the right contents for your advertisements, with voices, music and sound effects conveying your message in the most appropriate way?

❑   Did you comply with the law in this field, reading and adhering to the Radio Authority's Code of Advertising Standards and Practice?

Running your campaign

❑   Did you purchase airtime only after discussing your schedule and advertisements with sales executives, and in as much depth as possible?

❏   Did you conduct a trial run to test your schedule and advertisements, measuring the responses to them in order to work out their plus and minus features?

❏   Was your schedule amended in the light of these findings, and continually updated to keep abreast of changing and developing circumstances?

❏   Were you a successful radio advertiser?

Appendix A: Independent radio stations

For easy reference, independent radio stations are categorized under the following headings:

England
Anglia Television Region
Border Television Region
Central Television Region
Granada Television Region
Harlech Television Region
London Television Region
TV South Television Region
TV South West Television Region
Tyne Tees Television Region
Yorkshire Television Region

Northern Ireland

Scotland
See under Border Television Region
Grampian Television Region
STV Television Region

Wales
See under Harlech Television Region

England

Anglia Television Region

Breeze AM, PO Box 300, Southend on Sea, Essex SS1 1SY.
Telephone: 01702 430966.

CN. FM 103, PO Box 1000, The Vision Park, Chivers Way, Histon,
Cambridge CB4 4WW. Telephone: 01223 235255.

Chiltern Radio (AM and FM), Chiltern Road, Dunstable, Bedfordshire
LU6 1HQ. Telephone: 01582 666001.

Essex Radio, Radio House, Clifftown Road, Southend on Sea,
Essex SS1 1SX. Telephone: 01702 333711.

Hereward Radio, PO Box 225, Queensgate Centre, Peterborough,
Cambridgeshire PE1 1XJ. Telephone: 01733 346225.

Horyon Radio 103.3, Chiltern Road, Dunstable, Bedfordshire LU6 1HQ.
Telephone: 01582 666001.

KCBC, Broadcast Centre, Centre 2000, Robinson Close, Telford Way
Industrial Estate, Kettering, Northamptonshire NN16 8PU.
Telephone: 01536 412413.

Mellow 1557, 21–23 Walton Road, Frinton on Sea, Essex C013 OAA.
Telephone: 01255 675303.

Northants Radio (AM and FM), Chiltern Road, Dunstable, Bedfordshire
LU6 1HQ. Telephone: 01582 666001.

Radio Broadland, St George's Plain, 47–49 Colegate, Norwich, Norfolk
NR3 1DB. Telephone: 01603 630627.

SGR FM, Electric House, Lloyds Avenue, Ipswich, Suffolk IP1 3HZ.
Telephone: 01473 216971.

Border Television Region

Manx Radio, PO Box 1368, Broadcasting House, Douglas, Isle of Man.
Telephone: 01624 661066.

Radio Borders, Tweedside Park, Galashields, Selkirkshire TD1 3TD.
Telephone: 01896 59444.

Central Television Region

BRMB Radio, Radio House, PO Box 555, Aston Road North,
Birmingham B6 4BX. Telephone: 0121-359 4481.

Beacon Radio, PO Box 303, 267 Tettenhall Road, Wolverhampton
WV6 0DQ. Telephone: 01902 757211.

Buzz FM, The Spencers, 20 Augusta Street, Jewellery Quarter,
Birmingham B18 6JA. Telephone: 0121-236 6777.

Fox FM, Brush House, Pony Road, Cowley, Oxford OX4 2XR.
Telephone: 01865 748787.

Gem AM, 29–31 Castle Gate, Nottingham NG1 7AP.
Telephone: 01602 581731.

Leicester Sound FM, Granville House, Granville Road, Leicester
LE1 7RW. Telephone: 01533 551616.

Mercia Sound, Hertford Place, Coventry, Warwickshire CV1 3TT.
Telephone: 01203 633933.

Radio Harmony, Ringway House, Hill Street, Coventry, Warwickshire
CV1 4AN. Telephone: 01203 525656.

Radio Wyvern, 5–6 Barbourne Terrace, Worcester WR1 3JS.
Telephone: 01905 612212.

Signal Radio, Studio 257, Stoke Road, Stoke on Trent, Staffordshire
ST4 2SR. Telephone: 01782 747047.

Trent FM, 29–31 Castle Gate, Nottingham NG1 7AP.
Telephone: 01602 581731.

XTRA AM, Radio House, PO Box 555, Aston Road North, Birmingham
B6 4BX. Telephone: 0121-359 4481.

Granada Television Region

Marcher Sound, The Studios, Mold Road, Wrexham, Clwyd LL11 4AF.
Telephone: 01978 752202.

Piccadilly Radio (Gold and Key 103), 127–131 The Piazza,
Piccadilly Plaza, Manchester M1 4AW. Telephone: 0161-228 2442.

Radio City (FM and Gold AM), PO Box 194, 8–10 Stanley Street,
Liverpool L69 1DL. Telephone: 0151-257 5100.

Red Rose (Gold and Rock), PO Box 301, St Paul's Square, Preston
PR1 1BR. Telephone: 01772 556301.

Signal Cheshire, Regent House, Heaton Lane, Stockport, Cheshire
SK4 1BX. Telephone: 0161-480 5445.

Sunset Radio, 23 New Mount Street, Manchester M4 4DE.
Telephone: 0161-953 5353.

Harlech Television Region

Brunel Classic Gold, Lime Kiln Studios, Wootton Bassett, Swindon,
Wiltshire SN4 7EX. Telephone: 01793 853222.

GWR FM, Lime Kiln Studios, Wootton Bassett, Swindon, Wiltshire
SN4 7EX. Telephone: 01793 853222.

Radio WABC, PO Box 303, 267 Tettenhall Road, Wolverhampton
WV6 0DQ. Telephone: 01902 757211.

Red Dragon Radio, Radio House, West Canal Wharf, Cardiff CF1 5XJ.
Telephone: 01222 384041.

Severn Sound, Old Talbot House, 67 Southgate Street, Gloucester GL1 2DQ. Telephone: 01452 423791.

Swansea Sound, Victoria Road, Gowerton, Swansea SA4 3AB. Telephone: 01792 893751.

Three Counties Radio, Old Talbot House, 67 Southgate Street, Gloucester GL1 2DQ. Telephone: 01452 423791.

Touch AM, Radio House, West Canal Wharf, Cardiff CF1 5DP. Telephone: 01222 384041.

London Television Region
Capital Radio (95.8 FM and Gold), Euston Tower, London NW1 3DR. Telephone: 0171-608 6081.

Choice FM, 16–18 Trinity Gardens, London SW9 8DR. Telephone: 0171-738 7969.

Classic FM, Academic House, 24–28 Oval Road, London NW1 7DQ. Telephone: 0171-284 3000.

Jazz FM, The Jazz House, 26–27 Castlereagh Street, London W1H 5YR. Telephone: 0171-700 4100.

Kiss 100 FM, Kiss House, 80 Holloway Road, London N7 8JG. Telephone: 0171-700 6100.

LBC Newstalk 97.3 FM, Crown House, 72 Hammersmith Road, London W14 8YE. Telephone: 0171-603 2400.

London Greek Radio, Florentia Village, Vale Road, London N4 1TD. Telephone: 0181-800 8001.

London Talkback Radio, Crown House, 72 Hammersmith Road, London W14 8YE. Telephone: 0171-603 2400.

Melody Radio, 180 Brompton Road, London SW3 1HF. Telephone: 0171-584 1049.

RTM, 17–20 Tavy Bridge, London SE2 9UG. Telephone: 0181-311 3112.

Spectrum Radio 558, Endeavour House, Brent Cross, London NW2 1JT. Telephone: 0181-905 5000.

Sunrise Radio AM, PO Box 212, Hounslow, Middlesex TW3 2AD. Telephone: 0181-569 6666.

WNK Radio, 185b High Road, Wood Green, London N22 6BA. Telephone: 0181-889 1547.

TV South Television Region

Allied Radio, Broadfield House, Brighton Road, Crawley, West Sussex RH11 9TT. Telephone: 01293 519161.

Invicta Radio (FM and Supergold), Radio House, John Wilson Business Park, Whitstable, Kent CT5 3QX. Telephone: 01227 772004.

Isle of Wight Radio, Dodnor Park, Newport, Isle of Wight PO30 5XE. Telephone: 01983 822557.

Ocean Sound (Gold, Light and Power), Whittle Avenue, Segensworth West Industrial Estate, Fareham, Hampshire PO15 5PA. Telephone: 01489 589911.

Southern Sound, Radio House, Franklin Road, Portslade, Sussex BN41 2SS. Telephone: 01273 430111.

Two Countries Radio, 5–7 Southcote Road, Bournemouth, Dorset BN1 3LR. Telephone: 01202 294881.

TV South West Television Region

Devon Air Radio, The Studio Centre, 35–37 St David's Hill, Exeter, Devon EX4 4DA. Telephone: 01392 430703.

Galaxy Radio, 25 Portland Square, St Pauls, Bristol, Avon BS2 8RZ. Telephone: 01272 240111.

Orchard FM, Haygrove House, Shoreditch, Taunton, Somerset
TA3 7BT. Telephone: 01823 321001.

Pirate FM, Carn Brea Studios, Wilson Way, Redruth, Cornwall
TR15 3XX. Telephone: 01209 314400.

Plymouth Sound, Earl's Acre, Alma Road, Plymouth, Devon PL3 4HX.
Telephone: 01752 227272.

Radio 210 (Classic Gold and FM), PO Box 212, Reading, Berkshire
RG3 5RZ. Telephone: 01734 413131.

Tyne Tees Television Region

Great North Radio, Swalwell, Newcastle upon Tyne NE99 1BB.
Telephone: 0191-488 3131.

Wear FM, Forster Building, Chester Road, Sunderland SR1 3SD.
Telephone: 0191-515 2103.

Yorkshire Television Region

Aire FM, PO Box 362, Leeds, Yorkshire LS3 1LR. Telephone: 01532
452299.

Great Yorkshire Radio, PO Box 194, Hartshead, Sheffield, Yorkshire
S1 1GP. Telephone: 01742 738566.

Hallam FM, PO Box 194, Hartshead, Sheffield, Yorkshire S1 1GP.
Telephone: 01742 738566.

Magic 828, PO Box 2000, Leeds, Yorkshire LS3 1LR.
Telephone: 01532 452299.

The Pulse, PO Box 235, Pennine House, Forster Square, Bradford,
Yorkshire BD1 5NP. Telephone: 01274 731521.

Sunrise Radio FM, 30 Chapel Street, Little Germany, Bradford,
Yorkshire BD1 5DN. Telephone: 01274 735043.

Viking FM, Commercial Road, Hull HU1 2SG. Telephone: 01482 25141.

Northern Ireland

Classic Trax BCR, Russell Court, Claremont Street, Lisburn Road, Belfast BT9 6JX. Telephone: 01232 438500.

Cool FM, PO Box 96, Newtownards, County Down BT23 4ES. Telephone: 01247 815555.

Downtown Radio, PO Box 96, Newtownards, County Down BT23 4ES. Telephone: 01247 815555.

Scotland

See under Border Television Region.

Grampian Television Region

Heartland FM 97.5, Lower Oakfield, Pitlochry, Perthshire PH16 2DS. Telephone: 01796 474040.

Moray Firth Radio, PO Box 271, Inverness IV3 6SF. Telephone: 01463 224433.

NorthSound, 45 King's Gate, Aberdeen AB2 6BL. Telephone: 01224 632234.

Radio Tay, PO Box 123, Dundee DD1 9UF. Telephone: 01382 29551.

STV Television Region

Central FM, John Player Building, Stirling Enterprise Park, Kerse Road, Stirling FK7 7RP. Telephone: 01786 51188.

Max AM, Forth House, Forth Street, Edinburgh EH1 3LF. Telephone: 0131-556 9255.

Q96 Radio, 26 Lady Lane, Paisley PA1 2LG. Telephone: 0141-887 9630.

Radio Clyde (1 and 2), Clydebank Business Park, Clydebank G81 2RX. Telephone: 0141-306 2222.

Radio Forth, Forth House, Forth Street, Edinburgh EH1 3LF.
Telephone: 0131-556 9255.

West Sound, Radio House, 54 Holmston Road, Ayr KA7 3BE.
Telephone: 01292 283662.

 ## Wales

See under Harlech Television Region.

Please note that this appendix is based upon extracts from *British Rate and Data*; refer to Appendix E: 'Recommended reading', page 142. Details are reproduced with the kind permission of the publishers, Maclean Hunter Limited.

All information is believed to be correct as at 1 January 1996 but is liable to change. You may want to refer to *British Rate and Data* for additions, updates and fuller details.

Inclusion within this appendix does not necessarily constitute recommendation of the radio stations listed and you are urged to take commonsense steps and advice before advertising on any of them.

Appendix B: Rate cards

Radio - the right frequency

96.4 & 97.1 RADIO

FM		88	90	92	94	96	98	100	102	104	106	108
AM		540		600		700	800		1000	1200	1400	1600

Great music - golden memories
1152 - 1170 - 1251 AM/MW

R A T E

SPOT DURATION

60 SECONDS	**+80%**
50 SECONDS	**+65%**
40 SECONDS	**+30%**
20 SECONDS	**-20%**
10 SECONDS	**-50%**

The rates quoted are for a 30 second duration spot.
Other spot lengths are available and their costs, in relation to
the 30 second spot rate, are seen above.
Commercials longer than 60 seconds will be pro rata to the
60 second rate.

RATES PER 30 SECONDS FOR

AVAILABILITY LEVEL		4
0000-2400	A	£ 3
0600-2400	B	£ 4
0600-1800	C	£ 6
0600-1200	D	£ 10
1200-1800	E	£ 5
1800-2400	F	£ 1

Rates effective from 1st October 1995 and are exclusive of VAT. Any three hour D E or F timeb
200%. End of week advertising (Thursday, Friday, Saturday) may be selected at a 25% surcha

SGR FM

At SGR FM, we are dedicated to giving our audience the best. We play 'the best mix of music' from
the last twenty years or so, featuring the best of today's quality hits and the great records of the 80's
and early 90's with classic hits from the 70's.

SGR is designed for younger adults in the key 20 to 40 age group, but it reaches everybody. The style of
presentation is accessible, innovative, fresh and fun. But SGR is more than just the best music, it's great
entertainment. Our listeners stay tuned for exciting competitions with great prizes, for the latest local,
national and world news, regular sports news updates and the most up-to-date travel and weather reports.

And that's why SGR has become one of the top local radio stations in the country since it relaunched just
over 3 years ago. Simply the best, that's the SGR promise on 96.4 FM and 97.1 FM.

WEEKLY PROFILE

15-34	172,000
34-44	80,000

ALL ADULTS	504,000
MEN	247,000
WOMEN	257,000

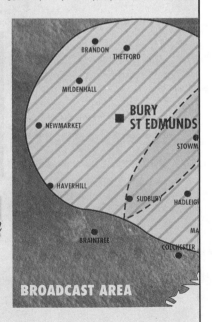

BROADCAST AREA

C A R D

1152 - 1170 - 1251 AM/MW

SGR FM AND AMBER RADIO

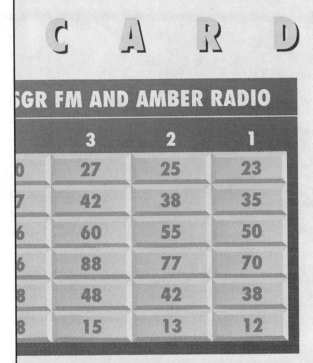

	3	2	1
0	27	25	23
7	42	38	35
6	60	55	50
6	88	77	70
8	48	42	38
8	15	13	12

...nd may be selected at a 25% surcharge, two hours 50%, one hour 100%, specified times
...ge.

AVAILABILITY LEVELS

All airtime orders will be made at the availability level in force at the time of booking. The levels vary due to the limited availability of commercial airtime. The more demand, the less airtime available, therefore, increasing the availability level. Booking your airtime well in advance enables you to enjoy the benefits of a much lower rate. Weekly availability levels will be issued upon request.

COMMERCIAL SCHEDULING

All spots will be evenly spread throughout the time segments of the campaign booked in order to reach the maximum number of listeners possible. Subject to availability, advertisers preferences will be considered but cannot be guaranteed.

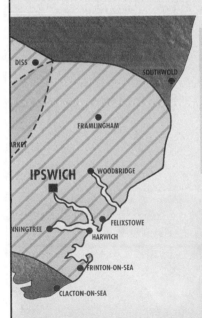

AMBER RADIO

AMBER RADIO puts you in touch with an older adult audience. It's 'easy-gold' music format is aimed at the over-40's but appeals to all ages who appreciate classic all-time hits from the past.

AMBER is a radio station for the 90's but brings back the musical memories with those great golden hits. It's Classic Hit Radio, with popular, familiar music of the last 35 years. From the Rock 'n' Roll years, through the 60's and 70's to the choice records of the 80's and 90's. All-time hits that all have that special quality that stands the test of time.

Quality presentation adds to the great entertainment. AMBER is warm and friendly, bright and alive, with a superb mix of music and information - offering an up to the minute service of news, weather, sport and travel reports 24 hours a day. AMBER RADIO - a mature sound for a sophisticated audience.

WEEKLY PROFILE

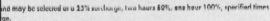

1152 - 1170 - 1251 AM/MW

35-44	80,000
45-54	85,000
55+	166,000
ALL ADULTS	504,000
MEN	247,000
WOMEN	257,000

TOTAL EAST ANGLIAN RADIO AREA

SGR FM, BROADLAND FM and AMBER RADIO together form East Anglian Radio, one of the most successful commercial radio groups in the UK.

SGR IPS & BURY	504,000
SGR COLCHESTER	132,000
BROADLAND FM	572,000
EAR TOTAL AREA	1,155,000
AMBER TOTAL	1,050,000

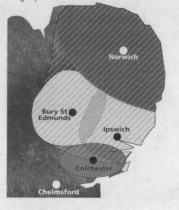

SGR IPSWICH & BURY **Radio House Alpha Business Park Whitehouse Road Ipswich Suffolk IP1 5LT Tel: 01473 461000 Fax: 01473 741200**

SGR COLCHESTER **Abbeygate 2 9 Whitewell Road Colchester CO2 7DE Tel: 01206 575859 Fax: 01206 561199**

BROADLAND FM **St George's Plain Colegate Norwich NR3 1DB Tel: 01603 630627 Fax: 01603 666353**

AMBER RADIO **Radio House Alpha Business Park Whitehouse Road Ipswich Suffolk IP1 5LT Tel: 01473 461000 Fax: 01473 741200**

VOLUME DISCOUNT

A series of volume discounts are available to advertisers who spend a minimum of £6,000 per annum and who give notice of annual expenditure in writing, in advance. Any shortfall in the agreed expenditure will lead to the airtime being re-invoiced at the actual level of discount achieved.

Please ask your representative for further details.

SPONSORSHIP AND PROMOTIONS

A number of sponsorship and promotional opportunities exist. These include - traffic and travel; weather and sports reports; tea and coffee breaks and the SGR FM and AMBER RADIO Roadshow. Full details are available on request.

CONDITIONS OF BOOKING

The general terms and conditions of contract for acceptance and broadcast of advertisements is available on request. All prices quoted are subject to VAT. This rate card applies only to outlets whose sole area of business is within the SGR FM and AMBER RADIO marketing area.

PRE-PAYMENT

Pre-Payment is required from all new and non-account clients.

CANCELLATION

Subject to the provision of the general terms and conditions (available on request) any bookings may be cancelled provided that notice in writing is given not less than 28 days before the scheduled broadcast date. Bookings may be cancelled within 28 days of broadcast subject to the following terms:

* 14 working days from date of broadcast, 10% of the total airtime value cancelled will be invoiced.

* 7 working days from date of broadcast, 20% of the total airtime value cancelled will be invoiced.

* 3 working days from date of broadcast, 40% of the total airtime value cancelled will be invoiced.

Unless a booking is cancelled in accordance with these conditions, an advertiser who fails to deliver advertisement copy will remain liable to pay in full whether or not any advertisement is broadcast.

Radio House Alpha Business Park Whitehouse Road Ipswich Suffolk IP1 5LT Tel: 01473 461000 Fax: 01473 741200

Why do so many companies who advertise on Capital Radio come back time and time again? It's simple, Capital Radio works.

95.8 CAPITAL FM

L O N D O N

R A T E C A R D

RATECARD

A STEP BY STEP GUIDE TO ADVERTISING ON 95.8 CAPITAL FM

Why do so many companies who advertise on Capital Radio - from the largest international businesses to single retail outlets - come back time and time again? It's simple; Capital works!

LONDON

London is a city with a population and affluence that other cities, indeed, some other countries, would find difficult to match. It's also home of the most desirable consumer group in the UK, with income per capita an astonishing 21% above the national average.

95.8 CAPITAL FM

95.8 Capital FM is London's most popular radio station and commands tremendous loyalty from its millions of listeners. It serves an area containing nearly 10 million adults; more than one fifth of the UK population. 95.8 Capital FM is particularly successful at reaching London's 15-34 year olds, with a high percentage of its audience in the ABC1 social class. Millions of Londoners couldn't imagine starting the day without the legendary Chris Tarrant's Breakfast Show. 95.8 Capital FM keeps London buzzing with its unique blend of chart music, entertainment, news and information, 24 hours a day, every day.

THE CAPITAL SERVICE

Whether you're a seasoned media veteran or have never advertised on radio before, you'll find that Capital's back-up service is second to none. Below we've outlined just some of the ways in which we can help you make the most of advertising on 95.8 Capital FM.

PLANNING

Our knowledge of when and where your target audience is listening to radio is unsurpassed. We have a sophisticated and proven planning system which will enable you to optimise your budget. You can buy individual spots based on our Ratecard Segments and Standard Rates (listed below) or, as most people do, book a series of commercials. In either case, our sales team will be happy to guide you through the process and ensure you reach your target audience effectively.

MAKING AN AD

Our professional, award-winning Commercial Production team can help with everything from recommending personalities for voice-overs, to writing, producing and recording an appropriate commercial. For more information, ring the team on 0171 608 6270.

RATECARD SEGMENTS			
Time Segment	Monday-Friday	Saturday	Sunday
P1	0700-1100	0700-1200	0900-1300
P2	0600-0700	-	-
	1100-1600	-	-
A	1600-2000	1200-1800	0700-0900
			1300-1900
B	2000-2400	1800-2400	1900-2400
C	0000-0600	0000-0700	0000-0700
	(M-F am)	(am)	(am)

STANDARD RATES						
	10"	20"	30"	40"	50"	60"
Ratio	(50)	(80)	(100)	(130)	(165)	(180)
P1	£1000	£1600	£2000	£2600	£3300	£3600
P2	£450	£720	£900	£1170	£1485	£1620
A	£325	£520	£650	£845	£1075	£1170
B	£150	£240	£300	£390	£495	£540
C	£25	£40	£50	£65	£83	£90

All prices shown are per spot and are exclusive of VAT at the prevailing rate. Spots in excess of 60 seconds can be bought in increments of 10 seconds and are charged pro-rata to the 60 second rate.

MARKET DATA

We have a wealth of general marketing data, which tells you about the potential of the market you're addressing and how 95.8 Capital FM can help your advertising exploit that potential.

DIRECT RESPONSE

For direct response advertising we can organise call-handling to collect names and addresses of customers, dispatch brochures or samples and provide further marketing data by building consumer profiles.

CAMPAIGN EVALUATION

We can organise pre- and post-awareness research for you, to show you exactly how much impact your campaign had, and to maintain optimum effectiveness for your future campaigns.

WHAT'S MORE...

We're committed to developing business in the Capital Radio area. For instance, we offer special rates to Local Advertisers and to those businesses or products new to radio and testing the effectiveness of the medium. In addition, our Sponsorship Department can help you make the most of the opportunities in this exciting area. Please ring us for more details of these and other incentives.

OUR PLEDGE TO YOU

We want your advertising to work! Here at Capital Radio London Sales we have unrivalled experience of planning radio. Above all, we appreciate the importance of responding with innovative plans and ideas that are unique to your brand or product. We'd be delighted to talk to you about your particular requirements so ring the Sales Department today.

0171 388 6801

CANCELLATION

Written cancellation or postponement requests for campaigns within 28 clear days before the scheduled broadcast date shall be considered by the Company and may be accepted at the company's absolute discretion subject to the following cancellation charges:

up to 28 clear days before the date of broadcast	40%
up to 14 clear days before the date of broadcast	60%
up to 5 clear working days before the date of broadcast	80%
day of broadcast	100%

COPY DEADLINES

Where advertisement copy is received less than 3 clear working days before the scheduled broadcast date, or is deemed not to have been so received as a result of failure to comply with the Company's technical requirements or submission or other procedures, the acceptance of such advertisement copy shall be at the absolute discretion of the Company and shall be subject to a surcharge of £75 per copy. In these circumstances the advertiser shall remain liable to pay in full for the advertising time whether or not it is broadcast.

TERMS AND CONDITIONS Our service is offered subject to our Standard Terms and Conditions, copies of which are available on request.

Why do so many companies who advertise on Capital Radio come back time and time again? It's simple, Capital Radio works.

1548 AM CAPITAL GOLD

L O N D O N

RATECARD

A STEP BY STEP GUIDE TO ADVERTISING ON 1548 AM CAPITAL GOLD

Why do so many companies who advertise on Capital Radio - from the largest international businesses to single retail outlets - come back time and time again? It's simple; Capital works!

LONDON

London is a city with a population and affluence that other cities, indeed, some other countries, would find difficult to match. It's also home of the most desirable consumer group in the UK, with income per capita an astonishing 21% above the national average.

1548 AM CAPITAL GOLD

With a transmission area that extends for over 30 miles in every direction from the centre of London, 1548 AM Capital Gold can be heard by nearly 10 million adults - that's more than one fifth of the UK population. Right from its launch in November 1988, 1548 AM Capital Gold has enjoyed tremendous popularity and success. The unbeatable combination of classic hits and live sporting action has made 1548 AM Capital Gold second only to its sister station 95.8 Capital FM, as London's most popular commercial radio station. All the greatest hits from the 60s, 70s, and 80s are presented by such household favourites as Tony Blackburn and Mike Read. What's more, the passionate coverage and commitment of Capital Gold Sport's service has made it the number one choice for true sports fans in the South East.

THE CAPITAL SERVICE

Whether you're a seasoned media veteran or have never advertised on radio before, you'll find that Capital's back-up service is second to none. Below we've outlined just some of the ways in which we can help you make the most of advertising on 1548 AM Capital Gold.

PLANNING

Our knowledge of when and where your target audience is listening to radio is unsurpassed. We have a sophisticated and proven planning system which will enable you to optimise your budget. You can buy individual spots based on our Ratecard Segments and Standard Rates (listed below) or, as most people do, book a series of commercials. In either case, our sales team will be happy to guide you through the process and ensure you reach your target audience effectively.

RATECARD SEGMENTS

Time Segment	Monday-Friday	Saturday	Sunday
P1	0700-1100	0700-1200	0900-1300
P2	0600-0700	-	-
	1100-1600	-	-
A	1600-2000	1200-1800	0700-0900
			1300-1900
B	2000-2400	1800-2400	1900-2400
C	0000-0600	0000-0700	0000-0700
	(M-F am)	(am)	(am)

STANDARD RATES

	10"	20"	30"	40"	50"	60"
Ratio	(50)	(80)	(100)	(130)	(165)	(180)
P1	£375	£600	£750	£975	£1238	£1350
P2	£250	£400	£500	£650	£825	£900
A	£108	£172	£215	£280	£355	£387
B	£30	£48	£60	£78	£99	£108
C	£10	£16	£20	£26	£33	£36

All prices shown are per spot and are exclusive of VAT at the prevailing rate. Spots in excess of 60 seconds can be bought in increments of 10 seconds and are charged pro-rata to the 60 second rate.

MAKING AN AD

Our professional, award-winning Commercial Production team can help with everything from recommending personalities for voice-overs, to writing, producing and recording an appropriate commercial. For more information, ring the team on 0171 608 6270.

MARKET DATA

We have a wealth of general marketing data, which tells you about the potential of the market you're addressing and how 1548 AM Capital Gold can help your advertising exploit that potential.

DIRECT RESPONSE

For direct response advertising we can organise call-handling to collect names and addresses of customers, dispatch brochures or samples and provide further marketing data by building consumer profiles.

CAMPAIGN EVALUATION

We can organise pre- and post-awareness research for you, to show you exactly how much impact your campaign had, and to maintain optimum effectiveness for your future campaigns.

WHAT'S MORE...

We're committed to developing business in the Capital Radio area. For instance, we offer special rates to Local Advertisers and to those businesses or products new to radio and testing the effectiveness of the medium. In addition, our Sponsorship Department can help you make the most of the opportunities in this exciting area. Please ring us for more details of these and other incentives.

OUR PLEDGE TO YOU

We want your advertising to work! Here at Capital Radio London Sales we have unrivalled experience of planning radio. Above all, we appreciate the importance of responding with innovative plans and ideas that are unique to your brand or product. We'd be delighted to talk to you about your particular requirements so ring the Sales Department today.

0171 388 6801

CAPITAL RADIO AND THE LONDON MARKET

London continues to be the country's most dynamic and exciting radio market, with Londoners having a greater choice of radio stations than anywhere else in the UK. We are delighted that the latest RAJAR results confirm 95.8 Capital FM and 1548 AM Capital Gold as London's favourite radio stations. This book features a selection of some of the most popular demographics to give you an idea of the size and quality of the audiences of both FM and Gold. If you'd like information on a specific target market please contact Capital Radio London Sales on **0171 388 6801**.

If you've got a product or service you want to advertise to Londoners then Capital FM and Capital Gold offer unrivalled numbers of listeners in all the important target demographics. It's simple, Capital Radio works.

95.8 CAPITAL FM AND 1548 AM CAPITAL GOLD

Capital Radio broadcasts to a huge area stretching 30 miles around Central London, covering over 12 million individuals - more than one fifth of the UK population. Every week almost 4.5 million Londoners, aged 4 years and over, choose to tune to either Capital FM or Capital Gold (a large proportion listen to both). What's more, these listeners spend an astonishing total of nearly 58 million hours tuned to Capital Radio.

	ADULTS	CHILDREN 4 - 14	MEN	WOMEN	ADULTS 15 - 34	ADULTS 15 - 54	ABC1s	HOUSEWIVES	HWS WITH KIDS	ABC1S 20 - 44
POPULATION 000s	9,829	1,694	4,773	5,057	3,845	7,018	5,391	5,077	1,466	2,779
WEEKLY REACH %	38	43	40	37	53	49	37	34	47	49
WEEKLY REACH 000s	3,761	733	1,903	1,858	2,054	3,429	2,020	1,717	688	1,361
AVERAGE HOURS	13.8	8.2	15.0	12.6	13.2	14.0	11.8	13.2	14.0	12.9
TOTAL HOURS 000s	51,979	5,996	28,625	23,354	27,067	48,052	23,871	22,647	9,651	17,546
SHARE OF LISTENING %	28.6	53.9	30.2	26.9	46.7	40.1	24.8	23.7	42.6	39.5

95.8 CAPITAL FM

In survey after survey 95.8 Capital FM remains the market leader. The brilliant mix of hit music, competitions, award winning news and entertainment has made it London's favourite since 1990. 95.8 Capital FM is central to the lives of millions of Londoners who wake up to the legendary Chris Tarrant's Breakfast Show and continue to tune in during the day. As the figures clearly show, FM has a huge and dedicated following amongst both London's kids and the important 15-34 age break. And you can't ignore the station's strong performance against upmarket ABC1s.

	ADULTS	CHILDREN 4 - 14	ADULTS 15 - 24	MEN 15 - 34	WOMEN 15 - 34	ABC1S	ABC1 MEN 20 - 44	HOUSEWIVES
POPULATION 000s	9,829	1,694	1,581	1,945	1,899	5,391	1,373	5,077
WEEKLY REACH %	33	39	52	48	53	32	46	29
WEEKLY REACH 000s	3,211	660	819	934	1,007	1,746	631	1,449
AVERAGE HOURS	12.3	8.4	11.4	13.3	11.6	10.3	11.8	11.8
TOTAL HOURS 000s	39,656	5,559	9,362	12,432	11,715	18,012	7,457	17,163
SHARE OF LISTENING %	21.8	50.0	45.0	39.2	44.7	18.7	30.8	17.9

ry's audience measurement system and uses methodology adopted by both Independent Radio and the BBC.

1548 AM CAPITAL GOLD

Since its launch in 1988 Capital Gold has been a success, attracting a large and loyal audience. Results from its first audience survey confirmed Gold's place as London's second largest commercial station and that's where it has stayed ever since. Gold's audience is concentrated among London's 25-54s who can't get enough of the station's classic hits from the 60's, 70's and 80's, presented by DJ's like Tony Blackburn, Alan Freeman and Mike Read. And for sports fans, Jonathan Pearce heads up the Capital Gold sports team delivering comprehensive live sporting action coverage in its own unique way.

1548 AM CAPITAL GOLD LONDON

	ADULTS	CHILDREN 4 -14	MEN 25 - 54	WOMEN 25 - 54	HOUSEWIVES	HWS WITH KIDS	C1C2S	C1C2s 25-54
POPULATION 000s	9,829	1,694	2,733	2,705	5,077	1,466	5,367	3,029
WEEKLY REACH %	15	11	23	18	13	19	18	23
WEEKLY REACH 000s	1,482	183	624	477	685	278	944	689
AVERAGE HOURS	8.3	2.4	9.9	8.6	8.0	7.8	8.9	10.7
TOTAL HOURS 000s	12,323	436	6,184	4,112	5,484	2,173	8,422	7,351
SHARE OF LISTENING %	6.8	3.9	11.0	9.7	5.7	9.6	8.5	12.9

AUDIENCE PROFILES

The tables below illustrate the sex, age and class profiles of the weekly audiences to Capital FM and Capital Gold, alongside those of the population of Capital's transmission area.

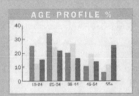

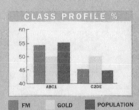

IN-CAR LISTENING

Talk about a captive audience! Radio, like no other medium, has the ability to reach and stimulate an audience whilst that audience is listening in-car. This is great news for advertisers, as the graphs below prove. They show the proportion of the adult audience to both Capital FM and Capital Gold that is listening in-car across an average weekday.

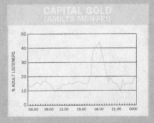

Data : All figures are taken from the Radio Joint Audience Research (RAJAR) survey covering the first quarter of 1995. Fieldwork took place over the twelve weeks between 2nd January - 26th March. RAJAR is the UK radio industry

PRODUCTION MENU

STARTERS

Our attentive staff will be happy to discuss your brief, quote for production, recommend appetisers for your audience or search for the right ingredients.

MAIN COURSES

Sound Bite -   Plain and simple. This filling treat contains a professional voice over, studio, script and materials. Very often it provides the basis for a more satisfying creation.
Cost: £400

Music Feast -   Using a Sound Bite base, the Music Feast spices up a more straight-forward advertisement with your choice of library music. Our extensive collection will have something to sate any appetite.
Cost: £500

Sound Supreme -   A real mouthful. The Supreme includes two professional voice over artists, who'll not only deliver your script but savour every nuance of it. It is accompanied by a selection of hand picked musical instruments, making this a good choice for anyone with a huge appetite for success.
Cost: £700

CHOOSE AN EXTRA!

A wide selection of extras are available to spice up your production. Additional toppings include:

Music - from £100 per track per ad.
Sound Effects - £10 each
Celebrity voice overs or jingles - price on application

Capital Radio Commercial Production - serving from 8.30am weekdays.
For reservations, call Gail, Phil or Jo on 0171 608 6270.

All prices quoted are exclusive of VAT @17.5% and are based on one commercial being transmitted on one IR station. Further usage fees may apply if the campaign extends beyond three consecutive calendar months, and in a small number of cases may apply after one month.

95.8 CAPITAL FM
LONDON

1548 AM CAPITAL GOLD
LONDON

"Immac's 1994 advertising campaign consisted of TV, radio and press. The total advertising awareness for Immac, amongst Capital and Kiss FM listeners, rose to a very satisfactory 66%. Additionally, over 27% of consumers said that the advertising made them think about trying the brand. This is the first time we have run a radio campaign for Immac and we hope to be able to build on it in the future."

Sue Brown
Brand Manager

IMMAC

CAPITALRADIOWORKS

95.8 CAPITAL FM   1548 AM CAPITAL GOLD

L O N D O N

CAPITALRADIOWORKS

BACKGROUND

Immac had previously used TV and press successfully. This time Immac wanted to test the effectiveness of radio in reaching its broad target market of women aged 15-34, and particularly in targeting young girls aged 12-16, to encourage them to try Immac as they were starting to think about hair removal.

It was felt that 95.8 Capital FM and Kiss FM could work powerfully with the young press titles Mizz, Big and Just 17, a theory which was put to the test by independent research carried out following the advertising.

THE CAMPAIGN

The main purpose of the campaign was to encourage young girls to sample the product on the basis that it was a more effective and longer-lasting method of hair removal than shaving.

Three commercials were produced taking humorous situations where legs treated with Immac proved to be vastly superior to legs that had been shaved. All three featured the strapline "no stubble, no trouble".

A total of 181 spots ran on 95.8 Capital FM achieving 640 Radio Ratings across 6 weeks, reaching 38% of 12-16 year old girls with an average of 17 opportunities to hear.

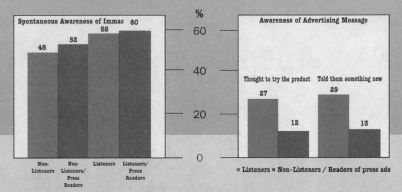

RESULTS

The research was conducted just after the campaign finished by Continental Research, using a sample of females aged 12-16.

- Spontaneous awareness of Immac as a hair removing product, at 58% amongst 95.8 FM Capital listeners, was 10 percentage points higher than amongst non-listeners (48%). Listeners who were also press readers scored higher still at 60%. However, amongst press readers who had not listened to Capital it was considerably lower at 52%.
- The difference in spontaneous awareness was even more marked amongst 12-14 year olds - 50% amongst Capital listeners as against 36% amongst non-listeners.
- Total awareness of Immac was 87% amongst listeners and 77% amongst non-listeners.
- Again, this difference was especially marked in the 12-14 year old group, with 83% awareness amongst Capital listeners but 66% amongst non-listeners.
- Perhaps even more significantly, the research showed that the radio advertising had had far more impact than the press. 27% of Capital listeners said that the radio ads had made them think about trying the product and 29% said that the ads had told them something new. However, the response from non-listeners who had read the press was much lower with 12% and 13% respectively.
- 44% of Capital listeners had received the message that Immac was more effective than shaving, with 59% understanding that legs would be smoother for longer.

CONCLUSION

The research showed that radio had achieved a substantial increase in awareness for the product and had played a crucial role in increasing the effectiveness of the press advertising.

Radio had also proved to be particularly effective in conveying the key messages of the campaign. There was a significant increase in the number of people intending to sample the product and the longer-lasting effect had been communicated well.

CAPITAL RADIO
L O N D O N

EUSTON TOWER · EUSTON ROAD · LONDON NW1 3DR · TEL: 0171 388 6801 · FAX: 0171 608 6150

"The Woolwich has always used radio in the advertising mix and we are happy to see the positive effects of a solus radio campaign. Increases in awareness were both through Continental's research and movement on the Gallup monitor. We certainly plan to continue to use radio, both through Capital and the rest of the independent radio network."

Chris Byrom
Marketing Manager

CAPITALRADIOWORKS

CAPITALRADIOWORKS

BACKGROUND

The building society market is extremely competitive, with many of the major organisations promoting similar products. The product ranges themselves can often seem complex and confusing, making the market as a whole seem unappealing to consumers. This makes for a tough environment for brand building.

The Woolwich was planning a campaign to promote mortgage services to first time buyers aged 20-29, and savings schemes to 30-40 year olds, targeting ABC1C2s in particular in both age groups. The campaign objective was to promote the products in a simple and memorable way while at the same time positioning The Woolwich uniquely as an approachable, friendly building society.

The Woolwich is one of the biggest supporters of commercial radio in the financial sector and was confident of Capital's ability to achieve broad coverage of the target market, so it was natural that Capital would form a substantial part of the media mix. In this case, it was decided to use this opportunity to quantify whether a new campaign could be successfully established on radio and subsequently transferred to other media.

THE CAMPAIGN

Monty Python's Eric Idle was chosen to make two light-hearted commercials of 60 seconds each, one for mortgage services and the other for savings schemes. Although the commercials had different lyrics and dialogue they both used the same creative approach.

The campaign ran for 3 weeks with 183 spots on 95.8 Capital FM and 1848 AM Capital Gold, achieving a 46% reach of ABC1C2 15-44s with a frequency of 7.9. Additional airtime was bought on LBC and JFM.

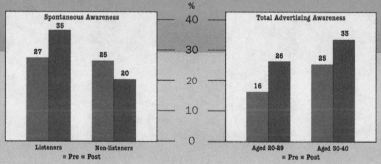

RESULTS

The results from Continental Research's panel of ABC1C2 adults aged 20-40 in London showed:

- Spontaneous awareness of The Woolwich as a provider of mortgage services increased from 27% to 35% among listeners and fell from 25% to 20% among non-listeners.

- Spontaneous awareness for the savings campaign among adult listeners aged 30-40 increased from 30% to 36%.

- Total advertising awareness among Capital listeners aged 20-29 increased from 16% to 26%, while awareness among listeners aged 30-40 increased from 25% to 33%.

CONCLUSION

The campaign was so successful that a second burst of advertising was placed on Capital and the creative treatment was extended to TV, thus achieving its important objective of establishing a new advertising theme initially on radio.

CAPITAL RADIO
L O N D O N

EUSTON TOWER · EUSTON ROAD · LONDON NW1 3DR · TEL: 0171 388 6801 · FAX: 0171 608 6150

When looking at a local rate card, you will almost certainly have two main areas of concern – that their audience matches yours as closely as possible and that you can obtain the best deal in the circumstances. This two-part checklist may help to clarify your thoughts in both respects.

	Yes	No
Does its transmission area cover our customers' locations?	❑	❑
Does its audience resemble our own?	❑	❑
– in terms of sexes?	❑	❑
– with regard to ages?	❑	❑
– in relation to social grades?	❑	❑
– in respect of other characteristics?	❑	❑
Does its audience penetrate far enough into our customer base?	❑	❑
– in terms of sexes?	❑	❑
– with regard to ages?	❑	❑
– in relation to social grades?	❑	❑
– in respect of other characteristics?	❑	❑
In short, is this a good match?	❑	❑

Reading a rate card: an action checklist – part 1

	Yes	No
Are the advertising rates acceptable to us?	❏	❏
Can we advertise at the appropriate times?	❏	❏
Are any surcharges agreeable to us?	❏	❏
Are the discounts substantial enough?	❏	❏
Are the terms and conditions fair and reasonable?	❏	❏
Are the 'cost per thousand' figures all competitive?	❏	❏
– per thousand of the station's audience?	❏	❏
– per thousand of our customer base?	❏	❏
– per thousand of our customer base for different advertisements?	❏	❏
– in relation to any other calculations applied by us?	❏	❏
In essence, is this a good deal?	❏	❏

Reading a rate card: an action checklist – part 2

Appendix C: Code of Advertising Standards and Practice

It is essential that you are familiar with the Radio Authority's code of advertising standards and practice, especially when you are composing advertisements. To help you find the sections that are most relevant to you, the code is divided up as follows:

You are advised to read the 'Practice Notes' particularly carefully as these set out the do's and don't's of writing acceptable radio advertisements.

Introduction

(a) The Broadcasting Act 1990 ('The Act') makes it the statutory duty of the Radio Authority ('The Authority') to draw up, and periodically review, a code ('The Code') which sets standards and practice in advertising and programme sponsorship on independent radio.

(b) This is the Radio Authority Code of Advertising Standards and Practice and Programme Sponsorship which the Authority has adopted under Section 92(1)(a) of the Act, after appropriate consultation. The Code applies to all advertisements and sponsorship on radio services licensed by the Authority.

(c) Radio Authority licensees are responsible for ensuring that any advertising and sponsorship they broadcast complies with this Code.

(d) The Authority advises licensees on interpretation of the Code and monitors compliance by investigating complaints. It may direct advertising and sponsorship which does not comply to be withdrawn. In the case of a breach of the Code, the Authority may impose any of a number of sanctions.

(e) The Broadcasting Act 1990 reserves the right of the Authority to impose requirements which go beyond the Code's rules. The Authority is empowered to give directions to exclude not only categories of advertisement and methods of advertising or sponsorship but also individual advertisements – either in general or in particular circumstances.

The code

(f) The rules are divided into three sections. Sections A and B deal with standards for the presentation and content of advertisements. They are followed by seven appendices which deal with categories of advertisement which require particular detail. Section C deals with programme sponsorship.

(g) The main code rules are followed by 'Practice Notes' which offer further guidance on practical implementation.

(h) Many of the advertising rules are derived directly from statute. As a minimum, licensees should be familiar with the provisions of the Broadcasting Act 1990 and relevant consumer protection legislation.

(j) Licensees may receive additional guidance on interpretation of the Code from the Authority's Advertising Regulation staff.

(k) Advertisers, advertising agencies, independent producers or potential sponsors seeking further clarification of any of the rules should approach the radio station on which they wish to advertise or sponsor programmes.

Advertising principles

1. **'Advertisement'** in this Code refers to any item of publicity, other than a sponsor credit, broadcast in return for payment or other valuable consideration to a licensee.

2. Radio advertising should be legal, decent, honest and truthful.

3. Advertisements must comply in every respect with the law, common or statute, and licensees must make it a condition of acceptance that advertisements do so comply.

4. The advertising rules are intended to be applied in the spirit as well as the letter.

Sponsorship principles

1. **'Sponsorship'** in this Code refers to any item of publicity, other than an advertisement, broadcast in return for payment or any other valuable consideration to a licensee.

2. Editorial control of sponsored programmes must remain with the licensee.

3. All sponsor involvement must be declared so that the listener knows who is paying/contributing and why.

4. The sponsorship rules are intended to be applied in the spirit as well as the letter.

Copy clearance and pre-vetting
ADVERTISEMENTS

(a) **'Local'** clearance applies to advertisements which are broadcast only by a radio station or stations servicing one particular locality. Copy may be approved for broadcast by relevant station staff who are responsible for ensuring that it complies with this Code. Exceptions to this are the 'special categories' detailed at (d) below.

(b) **'Regional'** clearance applies to advertisements which are broadcast by a number of radio stations in any one region out of the following five: Scotland and Northern Ireland; the North; Midlands and East Anglia; London; the South, West and Wales. Copy may be approved for broadcast by nominated regional clearance executives who are responsible for ensuring that it complies with this Code. (For details of the breakdown of stations per region and for the names and contact numbers of regional clearance executives, please contact the AIRC on 0171-727 2646). Exceptions to this are the 'special categories' detailed at (d) below.

(c) **'National'/'Central'** clearance applies to advertisements which are broadcast nationally or in more than one of the five regions detailed in (b) above. Copy must be submitted for advance clearance to an organisation or person approved by the Radio Authority, i.e. the Broadcast Advertising Clearance Centre (BACC).

(d) **'Special Categories'** of advertisement (whether for broadcast locally, regionally or nationally) need particular care and require advance central clearance as detailed in (c) above. They comprise:

Consumer credit, investment and complex financial advertising;

Alcoholic drink;

Medicines, treatments and health (includes contraceptives, feminine hygiene, slimming products);

Government advertising (e.g. COI campaigns, anti-AIDS, anti-drugs);

Advertisements containing references to political or industrial controversy or to public policy;

Advertisements claiming environmental benefits;

Charities;

Religion.

(e) For central clearance, advertisers or their agencies may submit five copies of preproduction scripts to the following address:

BACC, 200 Gray's Inn Rd., London WCIX 8HF. Tel: 0171-843 8265. Fax: 0171-843 8154.

(f) For all clearances, scripts should be accompanied by the following details:

Advertising agency or production house name, address and telephone number;

Name of agency or production house executive responsible for BACC negotiations;

Name of advertiser;

Name of product;

Reference number (if applicable);

Title and length of advertisement;

Recording date;

Date of script;

Transmission area(s);

First transmission date(s);

Name(s) of voiceover artist(s);

Precise description of sound effects.

(g) Supporting evidence must accompany scripts which include any factual claims, e.g. sales claims, price claims, consumer credit, guarantees, free or special offers, competition details, testimonials, etc.

(h) For central clearance, scripts are usually cleared within five working days and, if acceptable, stamped and returned with a BACC clearance form which notifies the licensee of any special requirements (e.g. scheduling restrictions).

(j) For regional clearance, scripts are usually cleared within three days. Two copies of the script need to be sent to the regional clearance executive, accompanied as relevant by the material listed in (f) and (g) above, and may be sent by facsimile. The script will be returned stamped 'approved', 'approved as amended' or 'rejected for reasons stated' as applicable.

(k) Licensees or their sales houses must hold photocopies of clearance forms and approved scripts prior to broadcast. This is their only means of knowing that scripts have been cleared. Final recorded versions of commercials need not normally be sent to the BACC. They must be checked against approved scripts by the licensee(s) concerned.

SPONSORED PROGRAMMES

(l) The Authority does not require sponsorship proposals to be cleared in advance.

(m) Licensees must ensure that their sponsored programmes comply both with this

Code and with the Authority's Programme Codes.

(n) The Radio Authority's Advertising Regulation staff will give general guidance to licensees on sponsorship proposals if requested.

Section A: Presentation of Advertisements

Rule 1
Identification

Advertising breaks must be clearly distinguishable from programming.

Practice Notes

Licensees must ensure that the distinction between advertising and programming is not blurred and that listeners are not confused between the two. Advertisements which have a similar style and format to editorial must be separated from programming by other material such as a jingle/station ident or by scheduling in the middle of a break.

Particular care should be exercised if expressions and sound effects associated with news bulletins are used. Listeners must quickly recognise the message as an advertisement.

References to programmes in advertisements are only acceptable in advertisements for specific television or radio programmes and in advertisements placed by sponsors.

Rule 2
Exclusion and distribution

(a) EXCLUSION FROM SOME TYPES OF PROGRAMME

Advertisements must not be broadcast within coverage of a religious service, a formal royal ceremony or occasion or a programme designed for reception in schools, unless the programme is over 30 minutes in length.

(b) DISTRIBUTION WITHIN SOME TYPES OF PROGRAMME

i. Licensees must exercise responsible judgements when scheduling categories of advertisement which may be unsuitable for children and those listening to religious programmes. Particular care is required in the following categories: sanitary protection products, family planning services, contraceptives, pregnancy-testing services/kits, anti-AIDS and anti-drugs messages and solvent abuse advice.

[NB: For the purpose of this rule, the Authority considers that children are aged 15 and below. However, there may be exceptional circumstances when advertising messages may be targeted at those aged 12–15 (e.g. anti-AIDS information or sanitary protection)].

ii. Advertisements for alcoholic drinks, cigars, pipe tobacco, sensational newspapers/magazines or their content and violent or sexually explicit films must not be broadcast in or around religious programmes or programmes/ features directed particularly at people under 18.

iii. Advertisements by charity organisations must not be broadcast in immediate juxtaposition to programme appeals for donations or community service announcements.

iv. Advertisements by religious organisations for the purposes of categories (a), (b) and (d) of Rule 2 of Appendix 7 must not be broadcast in or around programmes principally directed at people under 18, or likely to be of particular appeal to them.

Practice Note

A sense of responsibility should be exercised where advertisements or their scheduling could be perceived as insensitive because of a tragedy currently in news or current affairs programmes, e.g. a commercial for an airline should be immediately withdrawn if a neigh-

bouring news bulletin featured details of a plane crash.

Rule 3
Prohibited categories

Advertisements for products and services coming within the recognised character of, or specifically concerned with, the following are not acceptable:

(a) breath-testing devices and products which purport to mask the effects of alcohol;

(b) the occult (excluding publications of general interest, e.g. newspapers or magazines whose editorial is unrelated to the occult but which includes regular horoscopes and/or occasional articles on the paranormal);

(c) betting and gaming (includes bookmakers, betting tips, gaming machines and bingo but excludes non-gaming machines and the social, non-gambling activities offered by organisations/clubs who may also hold gaming licences. Also excluded are advertisements for football pools and lotteries permitted under the National Lottery etc Act 1993 and the Lotteries and Amusements Act 1976 as amended (this Act does not extend to Northern Ireland) provided that advertisements are neither directed at those under 16 nor broadcast in or around programmes likely to be of particular appeal to them).

(d) escort agencies and the like;

(e) cigarettes and cigarette tobacco;

(f) commercial services offering advice on personal, consumer or medical problems (excluding solicitors) which are not operating with the approval of their Local Authority/Local Health Authority or are not otherwise approved in a way acceptable to the Authority;

(g) guns and gun clubs (excluding shops which sell guns provided there is no mention of this);

(h) pornography (including 'topshelf' publications and the like);

(j) products for the treatment of alcoholism;

(k) hypnosis, hypnotherapy, psychology, psychoanalysis, psychotherapy or psychiatry (excluding certain types of publication approved in a way acceptable to the Authority);

(l) advertisements for investments in metals, commodities, futures and options, securities which are not readily realisable, volatile or complex investments such as swaps and currency or interest rate instruments, contracts based on market indices, and such other categories which the Authority may from time to time consider inappropriate;

(m) advertisements for the issue of shares or debentures (other than advertisements announcing the publication of listing particulars or a prospectus in connection with an offer to the public of shares or debentures to be listed on the Stock Exchange or dealt in on the Unlisted Securities Market);

(n) advertisements recommending the acquisition or disposal of an investment in any specific company (other than an investment trust company listed on the Stock Exchange).

Practice Note

An advertisement for an acceptable product or service may be withdrawn if the Authority considers that a significant effect is to publicise indirectly an unacceptable product or service.

Rule 4
Presenter-read advertisements

(a) GENERAL

Station presenters (excluding those involved in news and current affairs) may voice commercials provided that they do not:

i. endorse, recommend, identify themselves with or personally testify about an advertiser's products or services (however, presenters may refer to their own appearance(s) at an event run by an advertiser provided that the words used do not endorse or recommend the product or service which the event is designed to promote);

ii. make references to any specific advertisement, (whether presenter-read or not), when in their presenter role;

iii. feature in an advertisement for a medicine or treatment.

(b) PRESENTER-READ ADVERTISEMENTS WITHIN PRESENTERS' OWN PROGRAMMES

Station presenters (excluding those involved in news and current affairs) may voice commercials within their own programmes provided that:

i. a proper distinction and clear separation is maintained between the programming material they deliver and the advertisements they read;

ii. the form of words and style of delivery do not imply that the presenter is endorsing the product or service advertised.

Rule 5
Unreasonable discrimination

A licensee must not unreasonably discriminate either against or in favour of any particular advertiser.

Practice Notes

Rule 5 is derived from.Section 92(2)(b) of the Broadcasting Act 1990. Licensees are entitled to refuse advertising they do not wish to carry for legal or moral reasons but they must not unreasonably discriminate against or in favour of an advertiser. For example, to accept a commercial from one advertiser and decline a commercial from another simply because their products are competitors would constitute unreasonable discrimination.

If an advertiser believes he has been unreasonably discriminated against and has been unable to negotiate a settlement with the radio station, he is entitled to approach the Radio Authority with all relevant and detailed information.

Rule 6
Product placement

Product placement in programmes is prohibited.

Practice Note

The gratuitous mentioning of brand names in programmes constitutes a form of indirect advertising and is contrary to this Code.

Section B:
Standards for
Advertisements

Rule 7
Misleadingness

(a) Advertisements must not contain any descriptions, claims or other material which might, directly or by implication, mislead about the product or service advertised or about its suitability for the purpose recommended.

(b) Advertisements must clarify any important limitations or qualifications without which a misleading impression of a product or service might be given.

(c) Before accepting advertisements licensees must be satisfied that any descriptions and claims have been adequately substantiated by the advertiser.

Practice Notes

'The Control of Misleading Advertisements Regulations 1988' define an advertisement as misleading if '. . . in any way, including its presentation, it deceives or is likely to deceive the persons to whom it is addressed . . . and if, by reason of its deceptive nature, it is likely to affect their economic behaviour or . . . injures or is likely to injure a competitor of the person whose interests the advertisement seeks to promote'.

Under the Regulations the Radio Authority has a specifiduty to investigate complaints (other than frivolous or vexatious ones) about alleged misleading advertisements. The

Authority will require the removal of an advertisement which it has found to be misleading and is empowered to regard a factual claim as inaccurate unless adequate evidence of accuracy is provided when requested.

Advertisements must not misleadingly claim or imply that the product advertised, or an ingredient, has some special property or quality which cannot be established. Scientific terms, statistics, quotations from technical literature, etc. should be used with a proper sense of responsibility to the unsophisticated listener. Irrelevant data and scientific jargon should not be used to make claims appear to have a scientific basis they do not possess. Statistics of limited validity should not be presented in such a way as to make it appear that they are universally true.

Simple 'puffery' is acceptable in descriptions of products and services, as listeners can easily recognise and accept it for what it is. Any factual claim, however, needs substantiation and advertisers should be encouraged to provide supporting written evidence if the claim is likely to be challenged. Particular care is needed with superlative claims, e.g. 'cheapest', 'best', etc.

Rule 8
Political, industrial and public controversy

(a) No advertisement may be broadcast by, or on behalf of, any body whose objects are wholly or mainly of a political nature, and no advertisement may be directed towards any political end.

(b) No advertisement may have any relation to any industrial dispute (other than an advertisement of a public service nature inserted by, or on behalf of, a government department).

(c) No advertisement may show partiality in matters of political or industrial controversy or relating to current public policy.

Practice Notes

(a) *The term 'political' here is used in a wider sense than 'party political'. The*

prohibition precludes, for example, issue campaigning for the purposes of influencing legislation or executive action by local or national government.

(b) *The term 'industrial dispute' here includes strikes, walkouts and withdrawals of labour by workers, lockouts by employers, disputes between managements and differences between rival trade unions, etc. which are connected with the employment, nonemployment or terms and conditions of employment of any individual group. It makes no difference whether a dispute is official or unofficial.*

Whilst it is unacceptable for a trade union to advertise for support in a ballot, advertising for members is not prohibited provided the advertisement itself is not politically or industrially contentious.

The Radio Authority will normally regard an advertisement as having 'any relation to any industrial dispute' when it considers it to be in furtherance of an industrial dispute or expressing partiality in relation to such a dispute. Announcements of the resumption of normal working following agreement between management and unions, or those concerned with public safety during, for example, a gas strike are not precluded.

(c) *The Act requires that advertisements do not contain any words or phrases which could create or reinforce public opinion on controversial political, industrial or public policy questions.*

Advertisements for newspapers which have an editorial stance in political or industrial affairs and current public policies are acceptable, provided the copy does not give any impression that a partisan point of view is being expressed. In practice, such advertisements either state facts and/or pose questions, e.g. 'Read our four-page story on the coal strike' or 'Will hospital services improve or deteriorate under new proposed legislation?'.

Advertisements which include references to any political, industrial or public controversy should be submitted for central copy clearance.

Rule 9
Taste and offence

Advertisements must not offend against good taste or decency or be offensive to public feeling.

Practice Notes

Standards of taste are subjective and individual reactions can differ considerably. Licensees are expected to exercise responsible judgements and to take account of the sensitivities of all sections of their audience when deciding on the acceptability or scheduling of advertisements.

The following points may help to ensure that offence is minimal:

(a) references to minority groups should not be unkind or hurtful;

(b) references to religious or political beliefs should not be deprecating or hurtful;

(c) special precautions should be taken to avoid demeaning or ridiculing listeners who may suffer from physical or mental difficulties or deformities;

(d) advertisements should avoid salacious or indecent themes and should not include any sexual innuendo or stereotyping;

(e)   advertisements must avoid offensive and profane language;

(f) productions with salacious titles and clips from them should be carefully considered. Although it is recognised that the use of audio clips from advertised productions should portray their true nature, particular care must be exercised when selecting such clips – those containing bad language or sexual innuendo must be avoided;

(g) care should be exercised when promoting songs which contain words and phrases not normally acceptable. Some record titles and extracts of songs could result in widespread offence.

Rule 10
Protection of privacy and exploitation of the individual

Individual living persons must not normally be portrayed or referred to in advertisements without their prior permission.

Practice Notes

Advertisements for books, films, and particular editions of radio or television programmes, newspapers, magazines, etc. which feature the person referred to in the advertisement do not need prior permission, provided the reference or portrayal is neither offensive nor defamatory.

In the case of generic advertising for news media, the requirement for prior permission may also be waived if licensees reasonably expect that the individual concerned would have no reason to object. Such generic advertising must, however, be withdrawn if individuals portrayed without permission do object.

If impersonations or soundalikes of celebrities or well-known characters are to be used, it is strongly advisable for advertisers to obtain advance permission.

References to, and portrayals of, people active in politics should be carefully worded; they can easily fall foul of the requirements of the Act that political matters must be treated impartially and that advertisements must not be directed towards any political end.

Rule 11
Superstition and appeals to fear

Advertisements must not exploit the superstitious and must not, without justifiable reason, play on fear.

Practice Note

An example of a 'justifiable reason' would be where the aim of the advertisement was to influence listeners to take action to improve their own and their families' safety or welfare. Creating the impression of a person under threat from fire could be acceptable, for example, if the advertisement's function was

*to persuade adult listeners to fit a smoke
alarm in their homes.*

Rule 12
Price claims

Advertisements indicating price comparisons
or reductions must comply with all relevant
requirements of the Consumer Protection Act
1987 (Section III) and Regulations made
under it.

Practice Notes

*Actual and comparative prices quoted must
be accurate at the time of broadcast and must
not mislead. Claims of 'lowest prices' must be
supported by evidence from the retailer that
none of his competitors sell the advertised
product or service at a lower price. Claims of
'unbeatable prices' or 'you can't buy cheaper'
must be supported by evidence from the
retailer that his prices are as low as his competitors.*

*All prices quoted in the advertisement should
include VAT except for business-to-business
and professional services where it must be
made clear in the advertisement that prices
are exclusive of VAT.*

Rule 13
Comparisons

Advertisements containing comparisons with
other advertisers, or other products, are per-
missible in the interest of vigorous competition and public information provided that:

(a) the principles of fair competition are
respected and the comparisons used are
not likely to mislead the listener about
either product;

(b) points of comparison are based on fairly
selected facts which can be substantiated;

(c) comparisons chosen do not give an
advertiser an artificial advantage over his
competitor;

(d) they comply with Rule 14.

Rule 14
Denigration

Advertisements must not unfairly attack or
discredit other products, advertisers or advertisements directly or by implication.

Practice Note

*Advertisers must not discredit competitors or
their products by describing them in a
derogatory way or in a denigratory tone of
voice. This is particularly important in comparative advertising. Whilst it is acceptable
for an advertiser whose product has a demon-
strable advantage over a competitor to point
this out, care must be taken to ensure that the
competitor product is not depicted as generally unsatisfactory or inferior.*

Rule 15
Testimonials

(a) Testimonials must be genuine and must
not be misleading.

(b) Licensees must obtain satisfactory docu-
mentary evidence in support of any testimonial or claim before accepting it for
inclusion in an advertisement.

(c) Celebrities must not personally testify
about a medicine or treatment.

(d) Children must not testify about any product or service.

Practice Notes

*An expression of view or statement of experi-
ence of a real person in an advertisement is
regarded as a testimonial.*

*A person's professional status may be used to
lend authority to his/her opinions, e.g. 'I'm
Miss X, actress and model, and I use Y soap
because I think it's the creamiest'.*

*Celebrities may testify about products and
services they use but must not present,
endorse, recommend or personally testify
about any medicine or treatment. They may,
however, be the voiceover in an advertisement for a medicine or treatment if they are
merely playing a role or speaking commen-
tary.*

Station presenters may not testify on their own station about any products or services they use.

Fictional playlets (i.e. where characters express, in dramatised form, the claims of an advertiser) are acceptable, provided it is made clear that the situation and people depicted are not real.

Rule 16
Guarantees

Advertisements must not contain the words 'guarantee', 'guaranteed', 'warranty' or 'warranted', or words with similar meaning, unless the licensee is satisfied that the terms of the guarantee are available for inspection if required and are outlined in the advertisement or are made available to the purchaser in writing at the point of sale or with the products.

Practice Notes

It is illegal for any guarantee to diminish the statutory or common law rights of the purchaser. A guarantee must include details of the remedial action open to the purchaser.

Use of the word 'guarantee' etc. is valid in advertisements when a material remedial action is offered to the purchaser in addition to legal requirements or accepted trade practice.

The colloquial use of the word 'guarantee' may be acceptable in contexts where its meaning cannot be construed as being part of an advertiser's offer.

Rule 17
Use of the word 'Free'

Advertisements must not describe products or samples as 'free' unless they are supplied at no cost or no extra cost (other than postage or carriage) to the recipient.

Practice Note

A trial may be described as 'free' provided that any subsequent financial obligations of the customer are specified in the advertisement, e.g. the cost of returning the products

in the case of dissatisfaction or the cost of the products at the end of the trial period.

Rule 18
Competitions

Advertisements inviting listeners to take part in competitions are acceptable, subject to Part III of the Lotteries and Amusements Act 1976 (which excludes Northern Ireland).

Practice Notes

Licensees must be satisfied that prospective entrants can obtain printed details of a competition, including announcement of results and distribution of prizes.

Under the 1990 Act, there are no limitations on prize values.

Please see also competition rules in Appendices 2, 3 and 4.

Rule 19
Premium rate telephone services

Advertisements for premium rate telephone services must comply with the ICSTIS (Independent Committee for the Supervision of Standards of Telephone Information Services) Code of Practice.

In particular

(a) pricing information should be given as 'Calls cost xp per minute cheap rate and xp per minute at all other times' or as the total maximum cost of the complete message or service to the consumer;

(b) the identity of either the service provider or the information provider must be stated in the advertisement;

(c) the address of either the service provider or the information provider must be stated in the advertisement unless licensees keep on file the relevant address and broadcast the following announcement (at an appropriate time, twice a day) when advertisements for premium rate telephone services are being transmitted: 'Addresses of all premium rate telephone services advertised on (station name) are available to enquirers by telephoning (station number)'.

(d) advertisements for recorded message services which normally last over five minutes must include a warning that use of the service(s) might involve a long call;

(e) advertisements for live conversation services must state that conversations are being continuously recorded;

(f) advertisements should not encourage people under 18 to call live conversation services.

Rule 20
Matrimonial and introduction agencies

Advertisements from agencies who offer introduction services for adults seeking long-term companionship are acceptable, subject to the following conditions:

(a) before accepting advertisements licensees must establish that those wishing to advertise conduct their business responsibly and can provide a level of service commensurate with the claims in their advertising;

(b) the advertiser must conduct business from premises which clients, actual or potential, or other interested parties can visit. The full postal address, or published telephone number for that address must be included in all advertisements;

(c) licensees must obtain an assurance that the advertiser will not disclose data to a third party without the client's consent, and that the client's name will be promptly deleted on request;

(d) any quoted price must be the price at which the full service described in the advertisement is actually available and any qualification or supplementary charge must be made clear;

(e) advertisements must not:

   i. exploit emotional vulnerability by dwelling excessively on loneliness, or suggest that persons without a partner are in some way inadequate or unfulfilled;

   ii. contain material which could be taken to encourage or endorse promiscuity.

Practice Note

Agencies with computerised records must provide an assurance that they comply with the requirements of the Data Protection Act 1984.

Rule 21
Sexual discrimination

It is illegal (with a few exceptions) for an advertisement to discriminate against women or men in opportunities for employment, education or training.

Practice Note

The Sex Discrimination Acts 1975 and 1986 make it unlawful to discriminate solely on the grounds of sex. The Acts apply mainly to employment, education and training opportunities. There are a few exceptions; full details of which can be obtained from the Equal Opportunities Commission on 0161-833 9244.

Rule 22
Racial Discrimination

(a) It is illegal (with a few exceptions) for an advertisement to discriminate against ethnic minorities.

(b) Advertisements must not include any material which might reasonably be construed by ethnic minorities to be hurtful or tasteless.

Practice Note

The Race Relations Act 1976 makes it unlawful to broadcast an advertisement which indicates or implies racial discrimination. There are a few exceptions; full details of which can be obtained from The Commission for Racial Equality on 0171-828 7022.

Rule 23
Sound effects

Advertisements must not include sounds likely to create a safety hazard to drivers.

Practice Note

Caution should be exercised when considering distracting or potentially alarming sound effects such as sirens, horns, screeching tyres, vehicle collisions and the like; they may be dangerous to those listening whilst driving.

Rule 24
Direct marketing

Advertisements for products and services offered by direct marketing methods (e.g. mail order and direct response) are acceptable, subject to the following conditions:

(a) arrangements must be made for enquirers to be informed by the licensee concerned of the name and full address of the advertiser if this is not given in the advertisement – the address given to enquirers must be in a form which enables them to locate the premises without further enquiry;

(b) licensees must be satisfied that adequate arrangements exist at that address for enquiries to be handled by a responsible person available on the premises during normal business hours;

(c) samples of products advertised should be made available at that address for public inspection, if requested;

(d) licensees must be satisfied that the advertiser can meet any reasonable demand created by the advertising (e.g. via assurances of adequate stock);

(e) the advertiser must be able to fulfil orders within a certain delivery period which must be stated in the advertisement. This should normally be 28 days unless licensees are satisfied that there are particular circumstances where it is reasonable for the advertiser to state in the advertisement a delivery period in excess of 28 days;

(f) licensees must be satisfied that fulfilment arrangements are in operation whereby monies sent by consumers are only released to the advertiser on receipt of evidence of despatch (unless licensees are satisfied that adequate alternative safeguards exist);

(g) an undertaking must be received from the advertiser that money will be refunded promptly and in full to consumers who can show justifiable cause for dissatisfaction with their purchase(s) or with delay in delivery;

(h) advertisers who offer products and services by direct marketing methods must be prepared to demonstrate or supply samples of products to licensees in order that they may assess the validity of advertising claims;

(i) advertisers who intend to send a sales representative to a respondent's home or place of work must ensure that this intention is made clear either in the advertisement or at the time of response and that the respondent is given an adequate opportunity of refusing such a call. In the case of such advertising:

　i. advertisers must give adequate assurances that sales representatives will demonstrate and make available for sale the articles advertised;

　ii. it will be taken as prima facie evidence of misleading and unacceptable 'bait' advertising for the purpose of 'switch selling' if an advertiser's sales representative disparages or belittles the article advertised, reports unreasonable delays in obtaining delivery or otherwise puts difficulties in the way of its purchase with a view to selling an alternative article.

Practice Notes

Licensees must obtain assurances that advertisers with computerised records of respondents comply with the requirements of the Data Protection Act 1984.

Appendix 3, Rule 7 prohibits advertisements which invite children to purchase products by mail or telephone.

Appendix 1:
Financial Advertising

In this Appendix, 'investment', 'investment business', 'investment advertisement' and 'authorised person' have the same meanings as in the Financial Services Act 1986.

Advertisements for investment, complex finance and consumer credit should be submitted for central copy clearance.

Rule 1
Legal responsibility

It is the responsibility of the advertiser to ensure that advertisements comply with all the relevant legal and regulatory requirements.

Rule 2
Misleadingness

Advertisements must present the financial offer or service in terms which do not mislead whether by exaggeration, omission or otherwise.

Rule 3
Investment advertisements

(a) PERMITTED CATEGORIES

The following may be broadcast:

i.   investment advertisements issued by an authorised person, or those whose contents have been approved by an authorised person;

ii. advertisements issued in respect of the investment business of an authorised person, which are not themselves investment advertisements;

iii. investment advertisements which by virtue of the Financial Services Act 1986 do not require to be issued or approved by an authorised person.

Practice Note

Licensees may need to seek legal advice if an advertiser claims an advertisement should be considered:

i.   *not to be an investment advertisement;*

or

ii. *an investment advertisement which does not require to be issued or approved by an authorised person.*

(b) APPROVAL OF INVESTMENT ADVERTISEMENTS

Before accepting investment advertisements to which Section 57 of the Financial Services Act 1986 applies, licensees must be satisfied that:

i.   the compliance officer (or equivalent) of the advertiser, or authorised person issuing or approving the proposed advertisement, has confirmed that the final recorded version of the advertisement is in accordance with the Rules of the Securities and Investments Board (SIB) or the relevant recognised Self Regulating Organisation (SRO) or Recognised Professional Body (RPB);

ii. an investment advertisement or other advertisement in respect of investment business proposed by an appointed representative has been approved by the authorised person to whom that person is responsible.

Practice Note

Licensees may need to consult the relevant SRO or RPB or refer to the SIB concerning the compliance of any advertisement with Financial Services Act 1986 requirements.

Rule 4
Advertisements for deposit and savings facilities

The following deposit and savings facilities may be advertised:

(a) local government savings and deposit facilities in the United Kingdom, the Isle of Man and the Channel Islands;

(b) such facilities provided in accordance with the Building Societies Act 1986 by building societies authorised under that Act;

(c) such facilities provided by the National Savings Bank, and authorised institutions within the meaning of the Banking Act 1987;

(d) building society and authorised institutions' 'appropriate personal pension schemes' as established in accordance with the Social Security Act 1986;

(e) such facilities provided by registered Credit Unions regulated by the Credit Unions Act 1979;

(f) such facilities, guaranteed by the national government of an EC country, in currencies other than sterling, provided that a warning statement is included as to the effects of exchange rate fluctuations on the value of savings.

Practice Notes

Acceptance of advertisements in connection with deposit facilities is subject to any regulations made under Section 32 of the Banking Act 1987.

Rule 4 does not authorise the issue of any investment advertisement.

Rule 5
Interest on savings

References to interest payable on savings are acceptable, subject to the following:

(a) they must be stated clearly and be factually correct at the time of broadcast;

(b) calculations of interest must not be based on unstated factors (e.g. minimum sum deposited, minimum deposit period, or minimum period of notice for withdrawal) which might affect the sum received by individuals or be capable of misunderstanding in any other way;

(c) it must be made clear whether the interest is gross or net of tax;

(d) interest rates relating to variables (e.g. a bank's base rate) must be so described.

Practice Note

Attention is drawn to the code on the conduct of the advertising of interest-bearing accounts

adopted and implemented by the Building Societies Association, British Bankers' Association and the Finance Houses Association.

Rule 6
Insurance advertisements

(a) LIFE ASSURANCE AND DISABILITY INSURANCE POLICIES

Except with the prior approval of the Authority, such policies (not constituting investments) may only be advertised by:

i. companies authorised to carry on long term business under the Insurance Companies Act 1982;

ii. companies who have complied with Schedule 2F of the Insurance Companies Act 1982 in respect of carrying an insurance business or providing insurance in the UK;

iii. registered friendly societies under the Friendly Societies Act 1974 or the Friendly Societies (Northern Ireland) Act 1970 and authorised under the Friendly Societies (Long Term Insurance Business) Regulations 1987.

(b) GENERAL INSURANCE COVER

Except with the prior approval of the Authority, such cover (e.g. for motor, household, fire and personal injury) may only be advertised by:

i. insurance companies who carry on business under the Insurance Companies Act 1982, or have complied with Schedule 2F of that Act in respect of carrying on insurance business or providing insurance in the UK.

ii. Lloyd's underwriting syndicates.

(c) INSURANCE BROKERAGE SERVICES

Except with the prior approval of the Authority, general insurance, sickness insurance and other forms of long term assurance which are not covered by the Financial Services Act 1986 may only be advertised by:

i. brokers registered under the Insurance Brokers (Registration) Act 1977 or bodies corporate enrolled under that Act;

ii.   intermediaries who have undertaken to abide by the provisions of the Association of British Insurers Code for the Selling of General Insurance;

iii. building societies empowered to offer such services in accordance with the Building Societies Act 1986.

Rule 7
Insurance premiums and cover

Subject to any applicable legal requirement:

(a)   references to rates and conditions in connection with insurance must be accurate and must not mislead;

(b)   when specifying rates of premium cover, there must be no misleading omission of conditions;

(c)   in life insurance advertising, reference to specific sums assured must be accompanied by all relevant qualifying conditions, e.g. age and sex of the assured at the outset of the policy, period of policy and amount and number of premiums payable

Rule 8
Lending and credit advertisements

(a)   PERMITTED CATEGORIES

The advertising of mortgage, other lending facilities and credit services is acceptable from:

i.   Government and local government agencies;

ii.   building societies authorised under the Building Societies Act 1986;

iii. authorised or permitted insurance companies;

iv.   registered Friendly Societies;

v.   authorised institutions under the Banking Act 1987;

vi.   registered Credit Unions regulated by the Credit Unions Act 1979;

vii. those persons and bodies granted a licence under the terms of the Consumer Credit Act 1974.

Practice Note

Advertisers are reminded of the need for advertisements offering credit to comply with all relevant requirements of the Consumer Credit (Advertisements) Regulations 1989. Where there is doubt about the applicability or interpretation of these Regulations, advertisers should be encouraged to seek guidance from their Local Trading Standards department.

(b)   MORTGAGES AND RE-MORTGAGES

The following should be noted:

i.   advertisements for mortgages and remortgages are credit advertisements and the requirements of the Consumer Credit (Advertisements) Regulations 1989 therefore apply. Particular note should be taken of the requirements in these Regulations for secured loans;

ii.   advertisements for mortgages may, in some circumstances, also be considered as investment advertisements under the terms of the Financial Services Act 1986 and particular note should therefore be taken of the rules of the relevant SRO and RPB.

Rule 9
Tax benefits

References to income tax and other tax benefits must be properly qualified, clarifying what they mean in practice and making it clear, where appropriate, that the full advantage may only be received by those paying income tax at the standard rate.

Rule 10
Direct remittance

Advertisements are unacceptable if they directly or indirectly invite the remittance of money direct to the advertiser or any other person without offering an opportunity to receive further details.

Rule 11
Financial publications

(a) Advertisements for publications, including periodicals, books, teletext services and other forms of electronic publishing, on investments and other financial matters must make no recommendation on any specific investment offer.

(b) Advertisements for subscription services must be in general terms and make no reference to any specific investment offer.

Rule 12
Unacceptable categories of advertisement

Please see Section A, Rule 3.

Appendix 2:
Alcoholic Drink
Advertising

Advertisements in this category should be submitted for central copy clearance

These rules apply principally to advertisements for alcoholic drinks and low alcoholic drinks but the incidental portrayal of alcohol consumption in advertisements for other products and services must always be carefully considered to ensure that it does not contradict the spirit of these rules.

Rule 1
Distribution of advertisements for alcohol

Advertisements for alcoholic drinks must not be broadcast in or around religious programmes or programmes/features directed particularly at people under 18 (please see Section A, Rule 2).

Rule 2
Protection of the young

(a) Alcoholic drink advertising must not be directed at people under 18 or use treatments likely to be of particular appeal to them.

(b) Advertisements for alcoholic drinks must not include any personality whose example people under 18 are likely to follow or who have a particular appeal to people under 18.

(c) Advertisements for alcoholic drinks must only use voiceovers of those who are, and sound to be, at least 25 years of age.

(d) Advertisements for drinks containing less than 1.2% alcohol by volume must only use voiceovers of those who are, and sound to be, at least 18 years of age.

(e) Children's voices must not be heard in advertisements for alcoholic drinks.

Rule 3
Unacceptable treatments

(a) Advertisements must not imply that drinking is essential to social success or acceptance or that refusal is a sign of weakness. Nor must they imply that the successful outcome of a social occasion is dependent on the consumption of alcohol.

(b) Advertisements must neither claim nor suggest that any drink can contribute towards sexual success or that drinking can enhance sexual attractiveness.

(c) Advertisements must not suggest that regular solitary drinking is acceptable or that drinking is a means of resolving personal problems. Nor must they imply that drinking is an essential part of daily routine or can bring about a change in mood.

(d) Advertisements must not suggest or imply that drinking is an essential attribute of masculinity. References to daring, toughness or bravado in association with drinking are not acceptable.

(e) Alcoholic drinks must not be advertised in a context of aggressive, antisocial or irresponsible behaviour.

(f) Advertisements must not foster, depict or imply immoderate drinking or drinking at speed. References to buying rounds of drinks are unacceptable.

(g) Advertisements must not offer alcohol as therapeutic, or as a stimulant, sedative, tranquilliser or source of nourishment/goodness. While advertisements may refer to refreshment after physical performance, they must not give any impression that performance can be improved by drink.

(h) Advertisements must not suggest that a drink is preferable because of its higher alcohol content or intoxicating effect and must not place undue emphasis on alcoholic strength.

Rule 4
Safety

(a) Nothing in any advertisement may link drinking with driving or with the use of potentially dangerous machinery.

(b) Nothing in any advertisement may link alcohol with a work or other unsuitable environment.

Rule 5
Competitions and promotions

Alcoholic drink advertisements must not publicise competitions. Alcoholic drink advertisements must not publicise sales promotions which encourage or require multiple purchase.

Rule 6
Cut-price offers

References to 'cut-price/happy hour drinks', 'buy two and get one free', 'money-off coupons' and the like must be considered with extreme caution by licensees. Those references which encourage excessive or immoderate drinking are unacceptable. However, off-licences and alcoholic drink retailers may advertise price reductions for their stock.

Rule 7
Humour

Advertisements may employ humour but not so as to circumvent the intention of any of these rules.

Rule 8
Low alcohol drinks

Provided they comply with the generality of the Code and reflect responsible consumption and behaviour, advertisements for drinks containing less than 1.2% alcohol by volume will not normally be subject to rules 3(f), 4(b) and 5. However, if the licensee considers that a significant purpose of an advertisement for a low alcoholic drink is to promote a brand of stronger alcoholic drink or if the drink's low alcohol content is not stated in the advertisement, all the above rules are applicable.

Appendix 3:
Advertising and children

For the purpose of this Appendix, the Authority considers that children are aged 15 and below.

Rule 1
Misleadingness

Advertisements addressed to the child listener must not exaggerate or mislead about the size, qualities or capabilities of products or about the sounds they might produce.

Rule 2
Prices

Prices of products advertised to children must not be minimised by words such as 'only' or 'just'.

Rule 3
Immaturity and credulity

Advertisements must not take advantage of the immaturity or natural credulity of children.

Rule 4
Appeals to loyalty

Advertisements must not take advantage of the sense of loyalty of children or suggest that unless children buy or encourage others to buy a product or service they will be failing in some duty or lacking in loyalty.

Rule 5
Inferiority

Advertisements must not lead children to believe that unless they have or use the product advertised they will be inferior in some way to other children or liable to be held in contempt or ridicule.

Rule 6
Direct exhortation

Advertisements must not directly urge children to buy products or to ask adults to buy products for them. For example, children must not be directly invited to 'ask Mum' or 'ask Dad' to buy them an advertiser's product.

Rule 7
Direct response

Advertisements must not invite children to purchase products by mail or telephone.

Rule 8
Competitions

(a) References to competitions for children are acceptable provided that any skill required is appropriate to the age of likely participants and the values of the prizes and the chances of winning are not exaggerated.

(b) The published rules must be submitted in advance to the licensee and the principal conditions of the competition must be included in the advertisement.

Rule 9
Free gifts

References to 'free' gifts for children in advertisements must include all qualifying conditions, e.g. any time limit, how many products need to be bought, how many wrappers need to be collected, etc.

Rule 10
Health and hygiene

(a) Advertisements must not encourage children to eat frequently throughout the day.

(b) Advertisements must not encourage children to consume food or drink (especially sweet, sticky products) near bedtime.

(c) Advertisements for confectionery and snack foods must not suggest that such products may be substituted for balanced meals.

Rule 11
Children as presenters

(a) The participation of children in radio commercials is acceptable, subject to all relevant legal requirements.

(b) If children are employed in commercials, they must not be used to present products or services which they could not be expected to buy themselves. They must not make significant comments on characteristics of products and services about which they could not be expected to have direct knowledge.

Rule 12
Testimonials

Children must not personally testify about products and services. They may, however, give spontaneous comments on matters in which they would have an obvious natural interest.

Appendix 4:
Medicines,
treatments and health

With the introduction of new or changed products, the diverse licensing requirements of the Medicines Act 1968 and changes in medical opinion on particular issues, this Appendix cannot provide a complete conspectus of required standards in relation to health claims or the advertising of particular products or classes of medicines and treatments. The general principles governing the advertising of medicines, treatments and health claims (including veterinary products and services) are set out below.

Advertisements in this category should be submitted for central copy clearance.

Rule 1
Legal responsibility

Advertisements for products subject to licensing under the Medicines Act 1968 must comply with the requirements of the Act, Regulations made under it and any conditions contained in the product licence.

Rule 2
Claims

Claims about any type of product or treatment which fall within this Appendix require very close scrutiny. Whenever a proper assessment of such claims can only be made by a medically qualified expert, appropriate independent medical advice should be sought before acceptance. This includes claims relating to the nutritional, therapeutic or prophylactic effects of products such as food or toilet products.

Practice Note

The Radio Authority has access to a panel of eminent consultants* nominated by the leading medical professional bodies to advise it on health and medical aspects of advertising (*the Medical Advisory Panel – MAP). Medical claims in radio advertisements are referred by the Broadcast Advertising Clearance Centre (BACC) to members of this panel.

Rule 3
EC Council Directive 92/28/EEC

The above Directive concerns 'The Advertising of Medicinal Products for Human Use'

and has been implemented in the UK by The Medicines (Advertising) Regulations 1994 and The Medicines (Monitoring of Advertising) Regulations 1994. The latter Regulations require the Radio Authority to investigate complaints about alleged breaches of Regulation 8 of The Medicines (Advertising) Regulations 1994 and take appropriate action if necessary. The requirements of Regulation 8 are incorporated in the Rules of this Appendix.

Rule 4
Prescription-only medicines

Advertisements for medicinal products or treatments available only on prescription are not acceptable.

Rule 5
Products without a product licence

Advertisements for products which do not hold a product licence under the Medicines Act 1968 must not include medical claims.

Rule 6
Mandatory information

Advertisements for medicinal products must include the following information:

(a) the name of the product;

(b) the name of the active ingredient, if it contains only one;

(c) an indication of what the product is for;

(d) wording such as 'always read the label' or 'always read the leaflet' as appropriate.

Rule 7
Unacceptable references

Advertisements must not refer to the fact that a medicinal product has been granted a product licence or contain any reference to the European Commission or the Medicines Control Agency (unless the MCA require such a reference).

Rule 8
Medicines and children

Advertisements for medicinal products and treatments must not be directed exclusively or principally at children (i.e. those aged 15 and below).

Rule 9
Conditions requiring medical advice

Advertisements must not offer any product for a condition for which qualified medical advice should be sought or give the impression that a medical consultation or surgical operation is unnecessary (this excludes advertisements for spectacles, contact lenses and hearing aids).

Rule 10
Commercial services or clinics offering medical advice and treatments

Advertisements are only acceptable if the organisation wishing to advertise provides an assurance that it is registered with its Local Health Authority or is otherwise approved following referral to the Medical Advisory Panel (MAP). Central copy clearance is required.

Rule 11
Avoidance of impressions of professional support and advice

The following are not acceptable:

(a) presentations by doctors, nurses, midwives, dentists, pharmaceutical chemists, veterinary surgeons, etc. which give the impression of professional advice or recommendation;

(b) statements which give the impression of professional advice or recommendation by people who feature in the advertisements and who are presented as being qualified to do so;

(c) references to approval of, or preference for, a product or its ingredients or their use by the professions listed at (a).

Rule 12
Homoeopathic medicinal products

Advertisements for homoeopathic medicines are acceptable, subject to all relevant requirements of EC Directive 92/73/EEC on homoeopathic medicinal products.

In particular:

(a) advertisements are only acceptable for products which have been registered in the UK;

(b) product information must be confined to that which appears on product labelling (a statutory requirement). Advertisements may not, therefore, include medicinal or therapeutic claims or refer to a particular ailment;

(c) advertisements must include wording such as 'always read the label' or 'always read the leaflet' as appropriate.

Rule 13
Celebrities

Advertisements for medicines and treatments must not be presented by, or include testimonials from, persons well known in public life, sport, entertainment, etc.

Rule 14
Cure

Words or phrases which claim or imply the cure of any ailment, illness, disease or addiction as distinct from the relief of its symptoms are unacceptable. (Words such as 'help' or 'relieve' should be used.)

Rule 15
Tonic

Unless authorised by its product licence, the word 'tonic' is not acceptable in advertisements for products making health claims.

Rule 16
Unacceptable descriptions

Advertisements must not suggest that any medicinal product is a food stuff, cosmetic or other consumer product.

Rule 17
Diagnosis, prescription or treatment by correspondence

Advertisements must not contain any offer by correspondence (including post, telephone or facsimile) to diagnose, advise, prescribe or treat.

Rule 18
Self-diagnosis

Advertisements for medicinal products must not contain any material which could, by description or detailed representation of a case history, lead to erroneous self-diagnosis.

Rule 19
Guarantee of efficacy

Advertisements for medicinal products must not claim or imply that the effects of taking the product are guaranteed.

Rule 20
Side effects

Advertisements for medicinal products must not suggest that the effects of taking the product are unaccompanied by side effects. (It is acceptable to highlight the absence of a specific side effect, e.g. 'no drowsiness'.)

Rule 21
'Natural' products

Advertisements for medicinal products must not suggest that the safety or efficacy of the product is due to the fact that it is 'natural'.

Rule 22
Claims of recovery

Advertisements for medicinal products must not refer to claims of recovery in improper, alarming or misleading terms.

Rule 23
Appeals to fear or exploitation of credulity

(a) No advertisement may cause those who hear it unwarranted anxiety if they are suffering or may suffer (if they do not respond to the advertiser's offer) from any disease or condition of ill health.

(b) Advertisements must not falsely suggest that any product is necessary for the maintenance of health or the retention of physical or mental capacities (whether by people in general or by particular groups) or that health could be affected by not taking the product.

Rule 24
Encouragement of excess

Advertisements must not imply or encourage indiscriminate, unnecessary or excessive use of any medicinal product or treatment.

Rule 25
Exaggeration

Advertisements must not make any exaggerated claims, in particular through the selection of testimonials or other evidence unrepresentative of a product's effectiveness, or by claiming that it possesses some special property or quality which cannot be substantiated.

Rule 26
Comparisons

Advertisements for medicinal products or treatments must not suggest that the effects of taking the product are better than, or equivalent to, those of another, identified or identifiable medicinal product or treatment.

Rule 27
Analgesics

A 'tension headache' is a recognised medical condition and analgesics may be advertised for the relief of pain associated with it. However, no simple or compound analgesic may be advertised for the direct relief of tension. In such advertisements there must be no references to depression.

Rule 28
Food and beverages

Advertisers must ensure that their advertisements comply with all relevant legislation, in particular The Food Labelling Regulations 1984 and The Food Safety Act 1990.

Rule 29
Generalised health claims for food

Generalised claims such as 'goodness' or 'wholesome' may imply that a food product or an ingredient has a greater nutritional or health benefit than is actually the case. In some instances, reference to the properties of a particular ingredient may give a misleading impression of the properties of the product taken as a whole. Such claims are unacceptable unless supported by sound medical evidence.

Practice Note

Particular attention should also be paid to the requirements of the Food Labelling Regulations 1984, especially the prohibited and restricted claims set out in Schedule 6.

Rule 30
Dietary supplements

(a) Advertisements for dietary supplements, including vitamins or minerals, must not state or imply that they are necessary to avoid dietary deficiency or that they can enhance normal good health.

(b) Restrained advertisements for vitamins or minerals related to the dietary requirements of growing children, pregnant or lactating women or the elderly may be accepted subject to qualified medical advice.

Rule 31
Slimming products, treatments and establishments

(a) Advertisements for slimming products, treatments and establishments must be submitted for central copy clearance.

(b) Advertisements for slimming products and treatments must make it clear that weight loss can only be achieved as part of a controlled diet.

(c) Advertisements for establishments offering slimming treatments are acceptable only if such treatments are based on dietary control, which must be specified in the advertisement. Licensees must have obtained acceptable independent medical advice that the treatments are likely to be effective and will not lead to harm; and satisfied themselves that any claims can be substantiated. Any financial and other contractual conditions must be made available in writing to customers prior to commitment.

Rule 32
Sanitary towels and tampons

(a) Particular care is required when scheduling advertisements for sanitary protection products (please see Section A, Rule 2).

(b) Central copy clearance for advertisements for sanitary protection products is required.

(c) Copy must not contain anything likely to embarrass or undermine an individual's confidence in her own personal hygiene standards.

(d) Care must be taken to ensure that any detailed description of the product avoids anything which might offend or embarrass listeners.

(e) No implication of, or appeal to, sexual or social insecurity is acceptable.

(f) References to sexual relationships are best avoided.

(g) Female voiceovers are more appropriate than male ones and men should not feature prominently in advertisements.

(h) Particular discretion is required where an advertiser wishes to communicate a product's suitability to very young women.

(j) Comparative advertising is acceptable but commercials must not disparage other products, either directly or by implication.

(k) Normal marketing techniques are acceptable, e.g. pack offers, samples, etc.

Rule 33
Family planning services

(a) Particular care is required when scheduling advertisements for family planning services (please see Section A, Rule 2).

(b) Central copy clearance for advertisements for family planning services is required.

(c) Advertisements are acceptable only from family planning centres approved by a Local Health Authority, the Health Education Authority or the Central Office of Information.

Rule 34
Pregnancy-testing kits and services

(a) Particular care is required when scheduling advertisements for pregnancy-testing kits and services (please see Section A, Rule 2).

(b) Central copy clearance for pregnancy-testing kits and services is required.

Rule 35
Contraceptives

(a) Particular care is required when scheduling advertisements for contraceptives (please see Section A, Rule 2).

(b) Central copy clearance for advertisements for contraceptives is required.

(c) Advertisements must not promote or condone promiscuity.

Rule 36
Anti-AIDS and anti-drugs advertising

(a) Particular care is required when scheduling anti-AIDS and anti-drugs messages (please see Section A, Rule 2).

(b) Central copy clearance for anti-AIDS and anti-drugs messages is required.

(c) Advertisements are acceptable only from bodies approved by a Local Health Authority, the Health Education Authority or the Central Office of Information.

Rule 37
Refund of money

Advertisements must not contain any offer to refund money to dissatisfied users of any product or service within the scope of this Appendix (other than appliances or therapeutic clothing).

Rule 38
Sales promotions

Advertisements for medicinal products or treatments must not contain references to sales promotions (includes competitions, premium offers, samples).

Rule 39
Jingles

Jingles may be used but must not incorporate any medical/health claim.

Rule 40
Unacceptable categories of advertisement

Please see Section A, Rule 3.

(Reproduced by kind permission of the Radio Authority. Further information about this code can be obtained from: The Radio Authority, Holbrooke House, 14 Great Queen Street, London WC2B 5DG. Telephone: 0171-430 2724.)

Appendix D:
Useful contacts

Advertising Association, Abford House, 15 Wilton Road, London SW1V 1NJ. Telephone: 0171 828 2771

Association of British Chambers of Commerce, Tufton Street, London SW1P 3QB. Telephone: 0171 222 1555.

Association of British Market Research Companies, 67 Caledonian Road, London N1 9BT. Telephone: 0171 833 8251.

Association of Independent Radio Companies Limited, Radio House, 46 Westbourne Grove, London W2 5SH. Telephone: 0171 727 2646.

Association of Market Survey Organizations Limited, 16 Creighton Avenue, London N10 1NU. Telephone: 0181 444 3692.

Association of Media Independents Limited, 48 Percy Road, London N12 8BU. Telephone: 0181 343 7779.

Broadcasting Standards Council, 5–8 The Sanctuary, London SW1P 3JS. Telephone: 0171 232 0544.

CBD Research Limited, 15 Wickham Road, Beckenham, Kent BR3 2JS. Telephone: 0181 650 7745.

Department of Trade and Industry, Ashdown House, 123 Victoria Street, London SW1E 6RB. Telephone: 0171 215 5000.

Her Majesty's Stationery Office, St Crispins, Duke Street, Norwich, Norfolk NR3 1PD. Telephone: 01603 622211.

Incorporated Society of British Advertisers Limited, 44 Hertford Street, London W1Y 8AE. Telephone: 0171 499 7502.

Independent Radio Sales, 163 Eversholt Street, London NW1 1BU. Telephone: 0171 388 8787. And at: 8th Floor, Trafford House, Chester Road, Manchester M32 0RS. Telephone: 0161 876 5880.

Institute of Practitioners in Advertising, 44 Belgrave Square, London SW1X 8QS. Telephone: 0171 235 7020.

Maclean Hunter Limited, 33–39 Bowling Green Lane, London EC1R 0DA. Telephone: 0171 505 8000.

Market Research Society, 15 Northburgh Street, London EC1V 0AH. Telephone: 0171 490 4911.

Marketing Society, Stanton House, 206 Worple Road, London SW20 8PN. Telephone: 0181 879 3464.

Media Sales and Marketing, 365 Euston Road, London NW1 3AR. Telephone: 0171 383 3000. And at: 9th Floor, Portland Tower, Portland Street, Manchester M1 3LF. Telephone: 0161 236 8386.

Radio Advertising Bureau Limited, 74 Newman Street, London W1P 3LA. Telephone: 0171 636 5858.

Radio Authority, Holbrook House, 14 Great Queen Street, London WC2B 5DG. Telephone: 0171 430 2724.

Radio Joint Audience Research, 44 Belgrave Square, London SW1X 8QS. Telephone: 0171 235 7020.

Radio Sales Company, 32 Bedford Row, London WC1R 4HE. Telephone: 0171 242 1666.

Scottish and Irish Radio Sales Limited, 55 Broadway, London SW8 1SJ. Telephone: 0171 587 0001.

Appendix E: Recommended reading

Various publications may be of help and interest to you when planning, running and evaluating a radio advertising campaign. The following are likely to be especially relevant:

Books

A Practical Guide to Project Planning by Celia Burton and Norma Michael, £14.95. Published by Kogan Page Limited, 120 Pentonville Road, London N1 9JN. Telephone: 0171 278 0433. This is an extremely useful read for all prospective radio advertisers. It will enable you to assess your forthcoming activities in a full and effective manner.

The Effective Use of Market Research by Robin Birn, £12.95. Published by Kogan Page Limited, 120 Pentonville Road, London N1 9JN. Telephone: 0171 278 0433. A good book for anyone who is not yet wholly familiar with the dos and don'ts of market research. It tackles the subject in a clear and sensible manner which is easy to absorb and understand.

Researching Business Markets edited by Ken Sutherland, £19.95. Published by Kogan Page Limited, 120 Pentonville Road, London N1 9JN. Telephone: 0171 278 0433. This practical handbook is a first-class introduction to marketing research, describing all the various techniques and their particular strengths and weaknesses. It should enable you to become a more informed research buyer and user.

Budgeting by Terry Dickey, £9.99. Published by Kogan Page Limited, 120 Pentonville Road, London N1 9JN. Telephone: 0171 278 0433. A readable book which should help you in your financial planning for radio advertising activities. A sensible and informative buy.

Creative People by Winston Fletcher, £14.95. Published by Random House, 20 Vauxhall Bridge Road, London SW1V 2SA. Telephone: 0171 973 9670. This guide examines the relationships between creative people and their employers.

Check it out before dealing with those individuals who will be creating your advertisements!

Law and the Media by Tom Crone, £14.95. Published by Butterworth Heinemann Limited, Linacre House, Jordan Hill, Oxford OX2 8DP. Telephone: 01865 311366. An everyday guide for professionals which is sufficiently jargon-free and down-to-earth to be a first-rate addition to the would-be advertiser's book collection. It is worth referring to prior to advertising activities.

Magazines
Campaign. £1.85 for one copy, £85 per year. Published by Haymarket Campaign Magazines Limited, 22 Lancaster Gate, London W2 3LY. Telephone: 0171 413 4570. A weekly magazine which is the Bible of the advertising agencies and advertisers alike. This ought to be required reading for everyone entering the field.

Creative Review. £3.45 per single copy, £38 for one year. Published by Centaur Communications Limited, St Giles House, 50 Poland Street, London W1V 4AX. Telephone: 0171 439 4222. This is a monthly magazine that is worth checking out – it is full of fascinating articles and good advice which could help to improve your own advertising ideas.

Miscellaneous Publications
British Rate and Data. £130 per copy, £331 for one year. Published by Maclean Hunter Limited, 33–39 Bowling Green Lane, London EC1R 0DA. Telephone: 0171 505 8000. A 600-page directory published every month, and which includes in-depth details about the media in the United Kingdom. This is a must if you are to gain a reference source for every prospective advertiser. Check it out for up-to-date data on independent radio stations.

Please note that the books should be available from your local bookshop or library. Contact the appropriate publishers if difficulties arise. Ask for complimentary copies of magazines from the relevant publishers and subsequently take out annual subscriptions if you think they would be of ongoing use. All prices quoted are believed to be correct for 1 January 1996, but are liable to change in due course.

Glossary

The majority of terms used in this book are self-explanatory – advertising agency, transmission area and the like. Others are less so. They are given here.

À la carte agency. Advertising agency which produces advertisements but does not usually participate in media planning, negotiating and purchasing. Also known as a 'creative agency'.
Advance booking discount. Price reduction on advertising packages booked some time ahead of transmission.
Appropriation. Sum of money set aside for advertising activities. Better known as a budget.

Budget. See 'Appropriation'.

Combination discount. Price reduction available when advertisements are transmitted over two transmission areas.
Contract discount. Price reduction given to advertisers who spend a certain amount on advertising over a period of time. Also called 'expenditure discount' and 'volume discount'.
Cost per thousand. The cost of reaching every one thousand people within a station's transmission area.
Creative agency. See 'À la carte agency'.

Demographics. Study of the make-up of a population, by age, sex, social grade, etc.

Expenditure discount. See 'Contact discount'.

Fixing charge. Surcharge on advertisements transmitted at certain times.
Full service agency. Advertising agency able to plan and conduct an advertising campaign from start to finish.

Key. Identifying element specific to a particular advertisement enabling the response to it to be monitored accurately.

Media independent. Advertising agency which deals with the planning and purchase of advertising space and time. It does not offer creative services.

Package. Group of advertising spots purchased by an advertiser. A standard package would be 28 spots over a one-week period.
Penetration. The extent to which a radio station reaches an advertiser's target audience.
Profile. The make-up of a radio station's audience, by age, sex, social grade, etc.

Rate card. Sheet or pamphlet listing advertising and other data about a radio station.
Reach. Trade jargon for a radio station's estimated weekly audience.
Rep house. Independent sales organization which sells advertising time on behalf of radio stations. Services paid for by radio stations on a fee or commission basis. Also known as a 'sales house'.

Sales executive. Representative of an advertising agency or radio station.
Sales house. See 'Rep house'.
Social grades. Classification of the population based on the occupation of the head of the household.
Spot. Standard unit of advertising time, typically of 30 seconds duration.

Station-hop. Listeners' habits of re-tuning the radio from one station to another during advertisements.

Test market discount. Price reduction offered to first-time advertisers. Also called 'first-time discount'.

Volume discount. See 'Contract discount'.

Index